Selina Flavius is a London-based Senior Account Executive who created and runs the coaching platform Black Girl Finance. A conversation with a colleague about investing and financial goals prompted Selina to research how Black women fare when it comes to their money and finances – and, after reading the ethnicity pay gap statistics, was determined to help. She put her thoughts into action and launched her website and Instagram account in April 2019 to create a safe space for women to talk all things money. *Black Girl Finance* is Selina's first book.

Black Girl Finance

SELINA FLAVIUS

QUERCUS

First published in Great Britain in 2021 by Quercus Editions Ltd

This paperback published in 2022 by

QUERCUS

Quercus Editions Ltd
Carmelite House
50 Victoria Embankment
London EC4Y 0DZ

An Hachette UK company

The authorized representative in the EEA is Hachette Ireland,
8 Castlecourt Centre, Dublin 15, D15 XTP3, Ireland (email: info@hbgi.ie)

A CIP catalogue record for this book is available
from the British Library

PB ISBN 978 1 52941 428 8
Ebook ISBN 978 1 52941 430 1

10

Typeset by CC Book Production
Printed and bound in Great Britain by Clays Ltd, Elcograf S.p.A.

Papers used by Quercus are from well-managed forests and other responsible sources.

To my family,
Crismina, Colleen, Sian, Sonia, Dajan and Ray

CONTENTS

CONTENTS

INTRODUCTION

Have you ever googled 'personal finance books'? Try it. You'll see that the top-listed searches include *The Richest Man in Babylon* (1926), *Rich Dad Poor Dad* (1997) and Dave Ramsey's *The Total Money Makeover* (2003). In fact, of the top ten books that appear, all but two (well, one and a half – one of these was co-authored by a man) were written by men, and just two were written by people of colour.

I guess that makes sense; it is a fact that the global finance sector has always been, and remains to this day, very white and very male. There are more chief executive officers (CEOs) of FTSE 100 companies called Steve than there are CEOs from ethnic minority backgrounds, and more Davids and Steves than women *and* ethnic minorities put together. These facts should raise a red flag for everyone –

white men included. I'm a Black senior account executive with a natural interest in personal finance, and it makes me more than a little depressed. It got me thinking: where are the Black, female voices in finance, and how do we elevate them to the heights they deserve?

This is something I stewed over for a long time, until a conversation about investing and financial goals with one of my colleagues eventually pushed me to research how Black women fare when it comes to money and finances. Recent reports on the gender pay gap (GPG) and the ethnicity pay gap (EPG) make for pretty grim reading. In 2020, for every $1 a man takes home, a woman takes home 81 cents.* The 2019 World Economic Forum (WEF) report of global GPGs shows that there is no country without a gender pay gap, and the WEF estimates it will take 257 years to close this gap. What's more, a study carried out by accountant Price-waterhouseCoopers (PwC) revealed that British women would collectively earn £90 billion more every year if the GPG were closed. You read that correctly. I don't want to even try to work out just how much money women will be missing out on for the next 257 years.

The picture becomes bleaker still when we look at the

---

* https://www.payscale.com/data/gender-pay-gap

intersection of the gender and ethnicity pay gaps, which Black, Asian and minority ethnic (BAME) women find themselves doubly impacted by (it's not for nothing that we've all been told, 'You have to work twice as hard to get half as far'). A recent report by the Runnymede Trust shows that Black African and Bangladeshi households in the UK have only 10p of savings and assets for every £1 of white British wealth, and Black female graduates are paid on average 9% less than white female graduates – the equivalent of £3,000 a year.* This gap only widens over our lifetimes: with Black workers 8.8% less likely than white workers to be managers or directors in businesses, Black pensioner families receiving almost £200 less per week than white British pensioner families, and 1.2 million women retiring with no savings at all, it isn't hard to imagine how much worse off many Black women must be. Of course, these statistics were published prior to the Covid-19 pandemic, which has been predicted to set women's economic progress back half a century.† Many

---

* 2018 Resolution Foundation think tank. See https://www. resolutionfoundation.org/press-releases/black-and-ethnic-minority-workers-face-a-3-2bn-annual-pay-penalty

† According to warnings from international institutions including the World Economic Forum and UN Women: https://www.unwomen.org/en/news/stories/2020/9/explainer-everything-you-need-to-know-about-equal-pay

women work part-time and are assumed to be the carers at home – on average, women do three times as much childcare and looking after the home as men do, globally. Due to this, the GPG is predicted to widen even more.

Why does all this matter? Well, these pay penalties keep Black women down and make it so much harder for us to change our personal financial situations, which leads to a vicious cycle: the less money you earn, the less likely you are to have savings or investments and, by the end of your working life, you won't have a big enough pension to live on or any wealth to pass on to the next generation – and so it begins again. On top of that, research shows that money worries can have a negative impact on our mental health and relationships (money trouble is the most common reason for couples in the UK to divorce*). A lack of personal wealth can lead to women staying in unhealthy, abusive relationships because they don't have any other option. It's more important than ever to take our financial well-being seriously.

You'd think that since the UK economy is losing

---

* https://www.independent.co.uk/news/business/news/money-marriage-end-divorce-day-relationships-personal-finances-slater-gordon-a8147921.html

an estimated £2.6 billion per year due to discrimination against ethnic minorities,* the government would take action to change things. All of this data shows that immediate change is necessary, yet it is painfully slow to happen. It isn't yet mandatory for companies with over 250 employees to report their EPG, unlike the GPG, and while small steps are slowly starting to be taken in the right direction, it's clear that this situation will outlive us. We literally can't afford to wait for that day. So, what can we do *right now* to take control of our financial situation and improve our personal wealth?

Well, picking up this book is a good start.

Black Girl Finance – what?

I created Black Girl Finance because it's high time that Black female financial success started to be widely celebrated and championed. I'm passionate about empowering women to start unapologetically thinking and talking about money. We know that struggling alone, in silence,

---

* https://www.hrreview.co.uk/hr-news/diversity-news/economic-cost-discrimination-uk-economy-127-billion-year/110225

does not move us forward, yet we so often do ourselves the disservice of not congratulating ourselves when things go well, or not being upfront about our own ambitions and aspirations. Even just saying the word 'money' can make us uncomfortable. Go on, say it out loud. MONEY. How does it make you feel? Anxious, worried, uncertain? If so, that needs to change.

I want to challenge the negative mindset that holds so many of us back when it comes to our financial goals. I want us all to be comfortable talking about money. It's shocking how many of us feel inhibited by a voice in our head telling us that we can't do maths and that even thinking about our finances is beyond us. Don't let anyone – especially yourself – tell you that you can't handle this, because you 100% can (see Chapter 1).

From my own personal financial journey and from conversations with others, I know that women are *very* interested in money and their finances, even if they don't like to shout about it. That's why, after reading the statistics and feeling frustrated by the lack of diverse voices in this area of personal development, I decided to provide something for my community. In April 2019, I finally put my thoughts into action, took a web-design course and launched the online platform Black Girl Finance.

Black Girl Finance's aim is to create a community of unapologetic, ambitious, money-minded women. It's a safe space where we can have the confidence to start long-overdue, and often daunting, conversations about our finances. It started out as a four-step coaching service to help address the unique difficulties so many of us face in terms of our income and savings, and has evolved into a one-stop resource for all financial questions and concerns. As well as writing a blog, in which I highlight the latest information and data, I offer phone consultations to help my clients get a clear picture of their financial goals, put them into action and achieve them. I want to empower the Black Girl Finance community and give them the confidence to take control of their finances – and their futures.

Around the same time, I started curating a Black Girl Finance Instagram feed. To begin with, I wanted to highlight punchy quotes by female finance experts but, to my great disappointment, I couldn't find a single quote by a woman. This got me digging around harder, and I was delighted to find amazing and informative resources created by other women, which I then added to my website and social media. I've included a list of these remarkable women at the back of the book, so you can also be inspired and educated by them.

In 2020 I launched the Black Girl Finance podcast. Each week I take listeners through different aspects of personal finance, bringing in fantastic experts to share their tips and tricks. We have covered topics such as what to expect when speaking to a financial adviser, getting on the property ladder, saving and investing. I want to encourage listeners to take action, so my aim is to demystify the processes. Take the topic of speaking to a financial adviser: a large number of my clients have never accessed this service before, so if they have the good fortune to suddenly come into a large sum of money, they don't know where to start. I love hosting the podcast, because each guest has their own unique perspective and I learn so much from them. For example, if you listen to the episode that deals with insurance, you will hear my guest Rachel Kerr disagree with me, and I have to accept it, because she is the expert in her field. She knows what she's talking about, and I get a kick out of soaking up all this expert knowledge. I hope my listeners do, too.

Essentially, Black Girl Finance is my way of sharing the information I wish I'd had access to as I was growing up and heading out into the workplace. I would have advocated for myself more – and made fewer money mistakes – had advice like this been available, so I hope that my website, Instagram, podcast and now this book will help you to learn from my errors and start being more money-minded.

Black Girl Finance – who?

A little about me. I'm Selina, the founder of Black Girl Finance, the financial coaching platform and podcast. I grew up in a British Caribbean household where money was not a subject of conversation, apart from the save-for-a-rainy-day trope – more of that a bit later – so I had to learn the hard way how to handle money.

When we think of people who are 'good' with money, we imagine they're ridiculously quick at maths and have a weekly subscription to the *Economist*. I won't lie; it definitely helps if you know your way around a calculator. I got a B in GCSE Maths, which I'm pretty proud of, as it came after my teacher moved my entire class down a set after we got our mock results. I have never seen a teacher get so angry as he did that day. He screamed at us, thumped his fist on the desk and almost threw a chair. He was hopping mad. Let's be honest, if I had been in his shoes, I'd have probably also been peeved after spending a year preparing a class of pain-in-the-backside teenagers for an exam, only for them to get bad results. However, fast-forward to the real exam and I made a comeback. I knuckled down and studied diligently and managed to achieve the highest grade I could.

So I wasn't bad at maths (although later in life, when I was struggling with money, I constantly told myself I was). After getting my results I briefly considered studying economics at A level, but I quickly dismissed this idea. I now know many amazing female accountants and finance whizzes but, at sixteen, I knew none. Instead I opted for biology, chemistry and psychology, but my interest in finance continued to grow. I studied Oprah Winfrey and Warren Buffett relentlessly. I read books about them, their autobiographies, and books they had read, which – according to them – had changed their lives.

After sitting A levels, I went to university while also trying to raise my son. I'll be honest, I found this an extremely challenging time. I ended up dropping out, which is something I have struggled at times to talk about. But I came to realise that you don't need a degree to talk about money. You don't need a degree to do the maths, to work out your budget, to get on the property ladder, or to start investing. That's a myth, and one that's holding a lot of us back – which is why I'm here to bust it wide open.

After leaving university, I started a great career in business development (aka sales). I worked with amazingly ambitious men and women and, whenever I put myself out there and asked my boss, I got a pay rise. I never lost my interest in finances and – despite my pay increase – I started to realise that I wasn't applying the information I was learning to my own money. Although I had a good salary, with bonuses and shares, for a long time I lived from payday to payday (just like a lot of people I meet) and struggled with money. After hitting rock bottom financially, I knew I had to make major changes. I started by working on my mindset, then I moved on to the practical steps that are outlined in this book. I want you know: if I can turn things around, so can you.

Black Girl Finance – the book

The book you're holding is a personal finance guide written by, and for, Black women. It's for those of us who want to be considered, included, represented and catered for when it comes to conversations about personal finance. It's for women who are fed up waiting for society to include them. It's for you.

Picking up this book is a great first step if you want to take control of your finances. Whether or not you're aware of it, we are all on a financial journey. Our finances are an integral part of our lives and there's no escaping that fact. Will yours be a smooth financial journey, made up of conscious steps and controlled decisions, or will your journey be on a stormy sea, where you cover your eyes and pretend it's not happening? Since you're reading this book, I have a sneaking suspicion you want the former; you just have to turn the page to begin.

This book will give you the tools you need to take control and get you excited about your money. Each chapter delves into different aspects of your finances, from calculating your net worth to getting your head around saving and investing. Remember, I'm not a qualified financial adviser; all the information in this book is based on my own personal experiences and conversations I've had with experts and clients. I've written this book to share my advice and knowledge in the hope that it will benefit you. *I* certainly wish someone had advised me about it a lot sooner.

Throughout the book, I've included space for you to

write down your thoughts, exercises to help you work things out, and a list of helpful websites and recommended reading at the back of the book that will help you continue your journey. It's time to start making our hard-earned money work even harder for us.

Are you ready? Let's go.

1

MONEY MINDSET

To begin with, I want to get to the heart of what leads us to make financial decisions. To do that, we need to start examining our money mindset. Stop for a moment and think about when you started to handle money. I imagine you were quite young, right? If you're anything like me, you probably started handling cash at a young age, maybe when you were around eight years old. Perhaps you were given small amounts of pocket money by your family for special occasions or to reward good behaviour? That might not seem important for you to think about now, but research has suggested that our money habits are formed by the age of seven.*

_____

* https://www.telegraph.co.uk/finance/personalfinance/10075722/
Money-habits-are-formed-by-age-seven.html

It always amazes me that, even though so many of us handle money from a young age, by the time we get to our teenage years and early adulthood we lack the ability to talk about money. This is true for a number of women I've spoken to in the Black Girl Finance community, who say that, growing up, no one ever spoke to them about the best way to manage money, let alone how to save it and plan for the future. Money was simply not a topic of discussion. I grew up feeling that talking about money was inappropriate. I remember being around ten and asking my mum how much she earned at work. She gave me a cross look – no words were exchanged or needed. Without making a sound, she made two things plain: (1) that is none of your business, and (2) don't be so rude.

My mum was born in St Lucia and came to the UK as a teenager. Unfortunately, her relationship with her mother was difficult and, not long after they'd arrived in the UK, her mother kicked her out. This meant my mum had to grow up quickly and fend for herself from a young age. My mum worked hard, literally day and night, but I had older siblings at home who ensured I did my homework and ate dinner. At the weekend, my twin sister and I would go with Mum to Ridley Road Market to get the weekly shop, and every Sunday the family sat down for dinner together.

Mum was the epitome of the working mum. I'm not sure how much (if any) financial support my dad provided; my parents separated when my twin sister and I were very young and my mum never spoke about it. She handled the money and she made all the financial decisions. She did this silently, without any fanfare. She got on the property ladder, she sold up, she moved out of east London. She didn't speak about money – she simply got on with it. I have always looked up to Mum and admired her fierce work ethic, and I've tried to emulate this in my life.

My siblings and I were born in the UK and raised in a very working-class, very Caribbean household. We had Soca records and cabinets full of Caribbean trinkets, and for Sunday dinner we ate yams, dasheen, sweet potato or plantain (basically carbs with more carbs) with meat or fish. My mum, aunties and uncles spoke Creole or patois as well as English. They had two names (a name from back home and one for over here, or a house name and an outside name). We grew up immersed in Caribbean culture and traditions, while at the same time being British. You're probably wondering what any of this has to do with personal finance.

Well, even though we grew up with a rich dual-culture background, one message was clear: don't talk about money.

This is not a money misery memoir (if such a genre exists); our electricity was never cut off and our food never ran out, and my siblings and I had very happy, stable childhoods. My mum worked extremely hard to raise the five of us and, despite her humble beginnings and childhood hardships, she did great. That she hardly ever spoke about money is not surprising, really, if you think about it: without a parent to show her the ropes or hand down hard-learned financial lessons, she had to wing it on her own.

When it came to passing on her own wisdom to me and my siblings, the one thing she did advise was saving money in a pardner. In our community, a pardner (or susu) is a popular method of saving money that does not involve banks. It's a partnership you form with close friends to help you to save collectively, and it was created to provide access to capital when banks refused to lend to Black people (yep, you read that right). My mum was in a pardner with her friends, Monica and Ula from St Lucia (there may have been more, but they're the two I remember). Each person puts in a regular sum of money, which is entrusted to someone responsible, then the members of the pardner take it in turn to withdraw the pooled money collected each week or each month. For example, if each person contributes £50 per week and there are five people in the pardner, every week one person will receive £250. Who gets the pay-out each week or month is decided in advance.

So, while I heard Mum speak about her pardner, I didn't fully understand what it was until I was much older, and by that time setting up a pardner with friends was not generally considered to be an option (although pardners still exist – I was invited to join one recently, and I've also come across a Pardna app). The only explicit mentions of money at home had to do with the fact we went to a Catholic church – which is significant. Mother Teresa took a vow of poverty, so that might explain some of the things my mum used to say:

'Money doesn't grow on trees.'
'You can't take it with you when you're gone.'
'Rich people are cheats/fraudsters.'
'I only want enough to get by.'
'Money is the root of all evil.'

These messages shaped my mindset and thoughts about money. Maybe they sound familiar to you, too. With these in mind, have a think about the money messages you received while growing up. Try to recall any commonly used phrases or attitudes. When you needed money, who did you turn to? Were you taught that your dad handled all the money in the house? Or did you grow up in a house like mine where your mum was the head of the household? Or did you ask someone else entirely? Write down your memories in the space below.

_____

_____

_____

_____

_____

_____

_____

_____

_____

When we talk about a money mindset, we're talking our attitude to money. This is informed by the unconscious messages we absorbed as children that give us some insight into why we handle money in certain ways as adults. It's a complex subject. Some people who have experienced extreme poverty vow never to be poor again, and they take clear action with this goal in mind. Other people describe the poverty they experienced growing up: they believe that being poor is how things will always be, and that they will always struggle to make ends meet. The former person believes they can change things, regardless of where they began, while the latter person displays a very fixed way of thinking – a belief that nothing can change.

At the opposite end of the spectrum are people who are born into wealth or who inherit wealth. Some will continue to grow their money, whereas others will fritter it away and end up with nothing. Have a think about this for a second. Do any of these examples sound like you?

The aim of this exercise is not to assign or attribute blame to others in our past, but to acknowledge and recognise that all our experiences have an impact on our psyche, consciously or unconsciously. Watching my own mother work so hard, never taking time off for holidays, never eating out, rarely pampering herself and sometimes missing parents' evenings due to work, gave me the impression that you had to work long, hard, unsociable hours and never take days off (which explains why I always feel extremely guilty for calling in sick). My mum didn't work so hard so she could indulge herself or her kids; she did it because she had to. I look back on my childhood and feel like I wanted for nothing, but I know it wasn't easy – my twin and I qualified for free school meals and for uniform vouchers. I knew that, even though Mum worked hard, money was tight.

I subconsciously internalised the message that it was normal to work extremely hard for low pay, and you should never take days off or treat yourself, so that by the time I was a teenager and had started working, my feelings around money were negative and extremely disempowering. I was desperate to get my first job (which is great when you are a teenager), but as I got older and went on to start a career and have more financial responsibilities, it meant that I settled for jobs that paid me just enough to get by. I didn't feel worthy enough to put myself forward and ask for a pay rise; I had learned to crack on and make do. This meant that, as my cost of living increased and I bought a house and had a family of my own, my outgoings went up while my income stayed largely the same. As as result, I started to borrow money (I'll cover this later).

All of the above, coupled with a lack of knowledge about

22

personal finances, meant that, when I started working and earning a salary, I had no clue how to manage my money. I had no idea how to talk about money without seeming rude, and it felt greedy to desire more of it. I often spent all my salary, which meant being elated on payday then deflated and stressed out for the rest of the month when I inevitably ran out of money. As soon as I started to build my career, I fell into the dreaded cycle of living from payday to payday, regardless of how much I earned; if I earned more, I spent more.

I learned everything I know about money the hard way – through trial and error. It took a long time to adjust my money mindset, and this journey started when I became aware of my own negative and disempowering thoughts. My internal dialogue would say things like:

'I'm broke.'
'I can't afford it.'
'I'm no good at managing money.'
'I can't do maths.'
'I can't afford to save.'
'I don't understand investing.'
'Investing is for men in suits.'

But it wasn't until I heard myself say 'Money doesn't grow on trees, son' that I realised I had inherited a scarcity money mindset. That was when I knew that I was perpetuating negative money mindsets and, if I wasn't careful, I'd pass this mindset down to my son. We are what we continually tell ourselves we are. When I kept telling myself I was broke and I couldn't afford to save, the universe agreed with me: I was always broke and I had no savings (all I had was my Lloyds TSB overdraft – more on that later). I had to rewrite the script and change my narrative.

I had a similar breakthrough recently during a coaching call with a client, who works extremely hard at multiple jobs but hasn't built up the habit of saving regularly. I dug a bit deeper and asked how her parents handled money, and she recalled that her dad was very creative and quite relaxed when it came to money, and she recognised this attitude in herself. But she also had a desire to save up so she could treat family members who were extremely precious to her, so she wanted to change this trait. To make this happen, we started to work on rewiring her money mindset.

Whether our parents are workaholics or work-shy, we may either copy them without realising it or vow to never be like them. To change our money mindset, first we have to identify it and understand it. You have already examined the messages you picked up during childhood, but now it's time to examine any current negative money conversations you have with yourself. What kind of comments do you make about money to your friends and family? Take a moment and list them here:

_____

_____

_____

_____

_____

_____

_____

_____

_____

_____

_____

Once we start to think about it, we become aware of just how many of our attitudes are inherited. The messages we received as children are ingrained in us and can be extremely tough to shake. After you've had time to think about this, bring up the topic with friends and family to find out about their money mindset. I know that starting to have upfront conversations about money can be a challenge, but it's not impossible. If I can make the shift from not being able to talk about money to never shutting up about it, so can you!

It was a long journey for me. A few years ago, I was alone in my bedroom, sobbing, paralysed with fear, trying to deal with thousands of pounds of debt. I was unable to confide in my twin sister – in fact, I didn't tell a soul. I was embarrassed and ashamed, but I spent a lot of time pretending I was fine. Is it the British stiff upper lip? Or the Caribbean 'just get on with it' spirit? Whatever it is, we all seem to have become very good at pretending everything is okay – to our detriment. The stress of that period took its toll. I remember one particular day very clearly. I was feeling extremely anxious after spending all my money before payday, so I came up with a panicked plan to 'borrow' from my son's account. It felt wrong at the time, but it seemed to be my only option. I had borrowed £20 here and there often enough from my mum and my sisters, so I didn't want to borrow more. I believed that, had I tried to increase my overdraft limit, I would have been declined. To this day, this memory makes me so emotional and upset. I can still feel the shame and embarrassment, feeling that I had failed as a parent. (If you're wondering what I did, I ended up borrowing from my sister, but I didn't tell her how desperate or down I was about it.)

This was my rock bottom. This point was my catalyst for change. I didn't want to include this memory, but I want to be honest about how low things got for me so you know that if I can turn things around, so can you. At the time, I thought I was the only parent who had ever done this but I now know that, during times of financial hardship, just over a quarter of parents (27%) have dipped into their child's savings to pay a bill or put food on the table. Many of us are too ashamed to admit to or speak about these tough times, which is why it's so important that I create a safe space in which to have these conversations.

Fast-forward to the present, and I love talking about money. My sisters, mum and I get together regularly to talk about our finances; we have become a mini money squad! At our last money meeting, we discussed investing, which is something I never thought I'd say. Once you start having honest conversations with your loved ones about your money, you'll find it has a snowball effect and other people start to open up, too. It will mean that, rather than suffering in silence – as I did – you can support each other through your challenges and move towards your financial goals together.

I've had the same group of friends for years and we *never* used to talk about money. Now we're upfront with each other about our current goals. We challenge each other when negative voices come back out of the woodwork and we empower each other to strive for what we want to achieve. That's why I founded Black Girl Finance: my aim was to extend the same community of care to all my clients.

Now, go back to the last list you made and think about what you can replace those negative thoughts with. After a decade of telling myself 'I'm broke', I've completely stopped using that phrase (I've banned it from my vocabulary, and I don't let my clients or the people around me use it). Rather than telling myself I'm broke or I can't afford something, I ask myself: *how* can I afford it? What steps do I need to take to afford it? Similarly, instead of telling myself I'm bad at maths or not good with numbers, I simply whip out my trusty calculator and work it out. My brain wants to tell me I can't save or invest? No. How about, *how* can I save? *How* can I invest? Turning these thoughts around gives you back some power. Asking yourself these questions will push you to look at your numbers or ask someone else how they did it. You are not defeated but spurred into action. Creating new habits around money starts with taking baby steps.

Questioning and challenging negative thoughts about

money, instead of accepting them as truths, makes the biggest difference, because what you focus on can become your reality. Why would you even try to save or invest if you think you're broke all the time? Why would you try to create extra income if you think that money doesn't grow on trees? So, get rid of 'broke' today. Cross it off your list.

Now, take some time to think about a list of things you could say to counter your own negative beliefs about money.

_____

_____

_____

_____

_____

_____

_____

_____

_____

_____

I hope that doing this helps you to start changing your money mindset. Once you've done that, everything else will be a lot easier.

2

BUDGETING

If you are like me and have spent a long time not thinking about or examining your money habits, you'll probably feel overwhelmed by the task ahead of you. First of all, please be reassured that it's completely natural to feel this way. Don't beat yourself up, because you're definitely not alone. Second, fear not, because I'm here to break it all down for you, step by step. Grab a glass of wine and let's talk strategy.

Deciding to get your money in order is an important first step – but now what? First, you need to set yourself a budget. A budget is a financial plan that allows you to estimate your income vs expenses over a fixed period of time. Having a budget is essential for anyone who wants to manage their money. Too often we don't tell our money

31

where we want it to go, then we end up wondering where it went. Budgeting will help you to keep on track. Wouldn't that be a great position to be in – able to direct your income to the things that are most important to you? I hope you answered that question with a hearty 'yes'.

Now, I know a lot of people start to panic when they hear the word 'budget'; they think spreadsheets, they think maths, they think boring. To counter this, I focus on the many benefits of budgets. Budgeting gives you back control, helps you to prioritise paying your essential bills each month, and highlights any non-essential spending and where you're wasting money (why continue paying for that gym membership or TV package you never use when you can spend your money on something much more worthwhile?).

Paying bills – including your utility bills, mortgage, rent, loans, council tax, credit cards – is an essential part of life. Missing payments can result in serious consequences. No one wants to have their gas and electricity cut off or be visited by the bailiff. Going from month to month feeling overwhelmed about money causes stress and anxiety – but it doesn't have to be that way. So, how do you start budgeting?

The first step is to review your income and expenses. Grab a pen and your last three bank statements. In the space below, list your monthly income (including your take-home salary or wages, rental income, side-hustle profits, etc.).

Income

_____

_____

_____

_____

_____

_____

_____

_____

_____

Total income _____

Now it's time to start understanding your spending and work out your monthly expenses. This is probably the hardest task, as it requires you to go through your bank statements and write down every single expense. For expenses that vary from month to month, use the average cost over the last three months. To work out the average cost, take your last three months of expenses, add them up then divide by three.

Expenses

_____

_____

_____

_____

_____

_____

_____

_____

_____

_____

_____

_____

_____

Total expenses _____

Next, take away your total expenses from your total income. What do you get?

_____

Is your income high enough to cover all your expenses? Don't panic if it's not. The point of this exercise is for you to work out your income and expenses and to plan the next steps you can take. Budgeting was not previously a regular routine for me. It was only when I hit my low point that I realised I had to confront my spending habits. I had to take a long, hard look at where I was spending my money, which was uncomfortable, but necessary – and long overdue.

After I made my own list of my income and expenses, I found that the former was just about enough to cover the latter, but I knew I had to find a way to earn more or cut back on my spending, as I needed to clear my credit card debt. I had been dodging calls and letters from my bank for some time, so I called my bank to arrange a repayment plan for my credit card debt. My main focus was to ensure that I continued to pay my essential bills (mortgage, utilities, council tax, food) while at the same time addressing my debt. Over time, I have tested out a number of budgeting strategies, which I'll outline below. The key to effective budgeting is to do what feels right for you, as long as the method you use moves you in the right direction. The budget you choose should do three things:

1. Give you **clarity**: it should allow you to identify what you are currently spending money on and areas where you can make savings.
2. Provide **direction**: it should enable you to decide what you want to spend your money on instead.
3. Allow you to **focus** your money in the areas that are most important to you.

Budgeting helped me to eliminate stress related to my debt and unpaid bills, which had been hovering over me like a dark cloud. Budgeting was about a lot more than money; it was also about alleviating the anxiety I had felt for so long.

Now is the time to be upfront with yourself. Can you afford the lifestyle you're living? If not, can you cut back on non-essential spending or create extra income? This is where your budgeting strategy comes in. Here are three of the most popular options:

50/30/20

This is the strategy I recommend to most of my clients, as it's a simple, easy way to start budgeting effectively and it guarantees the three ingredients I mentioned above –

clarity, direction and focus. It requires you to assign 50% of your income to your essential Needs (such as utility bills, housing costs and food), 30% to your Wants (clothes, eating out and subscription services like Spotify and Netflix), and 20% to Savings. If you earned £2,000 each month, your budget would look as follows: £1,000 Needs (50%), £600 Wants (30%), £400 Savings (20%).

These percentages can be adjusted: for example, when I was planning my wedding, I halved my Wants percentage. Or perhaps you're saving to buy a car, so you might change this to 50% Needs, 10% Wants and 40% Savings. This is *your* financial journey – you will have your own goals that may mean you need to tweak your percentages. Of course, the two most important categories are Needs and Savings, so you must prioritise these each month. It makes much more financial sense to give up a meal out, a new outfit or a gym membership than it does not to pay an essential bill or take away from your future savings pot.

To start using the 50/30/20 method, use the space below to list everything you currently spend each month: your mortgage of £950 would go under Needs; your £50 spin class would go under Wants; and your pension contribution of £270 would go under Savings (check how much you pay into your workplace pension, if you have one).

Once you have listed all your monthly outgoings in the correct categories, add them up to get three totals.

Needs

_____

_____

_____

_____

Wants

_____

_____

_____

_____

_____

Savings

_____

_____

_____

_____

_____

Next, you need to work out whether your spending sits within the 50/30/20 percentages. Don't panic; it's easy to work out percentages and I'm going to walk you through it. First, make a note of your monthly take-home salary. Let's say it's £2,000. To work out 50% of your salary, you know you just have to divide it in two, but to make sure you're comfortable with working out percentages, let's do it the long way round. You need to divide 50 by 100 to get 0.5 (this changes the percentage into a decimal). Then, when you multiply 0.5 by your salary (£2,000 in this example), you get £1,000, which is 50%. This is the amount you should allocate for your Needs. Easy, right? So, to calculate 30% of your salary, repeat the process. To get the decimal, divide 30 by 100 (0.3). Multiply your salary by 0.3 and you get £600 to spend on your Wants. When you do the same for 20%, you get £400 for your Savings.

Now you're comfortable with percentages, work out the 50/30/20 allocation for your own salary. Once you've done that, compare those figures to the totals in your spreadsheet. Do the percentages match? If not, now's the time to crunch your numbers and see where you can make changes to get your proportions closer to 50/30/20 (remember, don't compromise on your Needs or Savings). It's a great way to tell your money where to go and keep your financial goals well on track.

CASE STUDY: BUDGETING

Client: Nicole

Nicole came to me because she was feeling overwhelmed by her finances. During our first call, Nicole explained that she had fallen behind on paying her rent and council tax, and she had other smaller debts outstanding. She said she knew that money was tight, but she didn't want to miss out on experiences for her and her family, so she hadn't prioritised some of her bills and was now in a financial mess.

The first thing I asked her to do was work out her budget. She couldn't remember the last time she had worked this out, but we needed to know immediately if her income was enough to cover her expenses. I was also concerned about her rent arrears and council tax, so I advised her that we should focus on this first: keeping a roof over her head was a priority.

She came back a week later and had completed a budget. When we discussed her budget in our second call, Nicole had worked out that she had just under £300 left each month after paying her expenses, including her essential bills (e.g. rent, council tax, food and utilities). She could afford her bills but, because she had not budgeted for a long time, it felt as if the opposite was true. Once she had seen the figures written down in black and white, she decided to set up direct debits for her rent and council tax so she would not miss payments again. She also had contacted her landlord to set up a repayment plan to tackle the arrears. Her budget showed her that she was actually better off than she had believed, so it had been worth reviewing her income and expenses. The pressure was now off and she knew where she stood. It was not a case of her not having enough money; instead, her money wasn't being directed to the most important areas. Nicole told me she felt a million times better after completing her budget: she felt reassured that she could afford all her bills.

Zero-based budgeting

With this method, every penny of income is accounted for and spent each month, meaning that you're left with a zero bank balance (income minus outgoings equals zero). If you are on a very tight budget, this is likely to be the best method for you, because you cannot afford to over-spend anywhere, so your spending needs to be mapped out precisely. It is also a good strategy if you are very detail-oriented, because you will be looking closely at where every penny goes.

Like the 50/30/20 strategy, zero-based budgeting allocates your outgoings into categories, but the difference is that here you're making sure that you spend every single penny you earn by the end of the month. First, tally up your income and expenses and work out the difference between them, looking at ways to scale back your spending if necessary. Then, group your outgoings into the categories that work for you (bills, food, travel, childcare, savings, miscellaneous, etc.). So, for example, if you earn £1,500 a month, everything you spend on Needs, Wants and Savings should total £1,500. If money is left over (perhaps a bill works out more cheaply than you had expected) you put it into Savings.

The benefit of this strategy is that it allows you to take control of your money down to the last penny. It gives you an increased level of scrutiny of your money, as it requires you to micro-manage your finances every single month. For some people, this is too time-consuming and fiddly, so this strategy isn't one I usually recommend to clients, but I'm including it here in case it works for you.

Envelope budgeting (or piggybanking)

This was originally a cash-based system, where you put money into different physical envelopes for different categories. Once the money in the envelope is spent, that's it. This strategy doesn't work for everyone, especially if you don't receive income in cash, but you can mimic the process by using the Saving Pots feature on Monzo or the Piggybanking method with Starling Bank. High-street banks are slowly catching up and are starting to update their apps to include savings pots, so look out for these. Envelope budgeting is the simplest way of setting money aside, but it doesn't give you a detailed overview of your spending habits.

These are just three of the budgeting strategies you could use, but there are many more if you do some research. No strategy will suit everyone, as we are all unique and do things in different ways, so try a couple and figure out which works best for you.

Like I said, I use the 50/30/20 strategy. When I started this, I called my creditor and set up a repayment plan of £100 per month to go towards my credit card debt of

£5,000. It was all I could afford, but I made repayments on time every single month for eighteen months, before I was in a position to make a balloon payment for the remainder of the outstanding balance. As soon as I set up the repayments and was working within my budget I felt at ease. Just taking this small step each month will take pressure off you and grant you the breathing room – and head space – to tackle further money goals and start to build up savings. A budgeting strategy should relieve your anxiety; if it doesn't, try another method until you find one that works for you. This is a non-negotiable step on your financial journey: having control of your finances is truly destiny-shaping. I'm excited for you to get started.

3

YOUR NET WORTH

You can't have a goal if you don't know where you're currently at: this is why you need to know your net worth. Don't be afraid of the term; it simply means your current financial situation. We often associate net worth with rich and/or famous people, and there are a lot of websites that focus on how much celebrities are worth. So, while 'net worth' might make us think of people who have a lot of money, it's not always true. If you've got a coin, you've got some net worth.

To get a snapshot of your personal net worth, you must first get past your fear of what you might find. It's true, your net worth might be lower than you'd like it to be, but you won't know until you check – and when you know, you can do something about it. It's important to note that your net worth can change over time, and you 100% *can* take action to change it. Remember, you're in control here.

Before I share how to calculate your net worth, I want you to promise that you won't beat yourself up if it's not as high as you would like. This might sound easy for me to say, but I can recall how I distraught I was the first time I calculated my net worth and saw a negative figure. This reaction is completely normal; acknowledge the feeling, but don't let it consume you. Remember, you're reading this book because you knew you had some work to do to improve your finances and get excited about them. This is a small, but necessary, part of your financial journey.

CASE STUDY: NET WORTH

Client: Maya

Maya wanted to have a coaching session to work out her net worth. This was something she hadn't thought about doing previously. Like many people, she had assumed it wasn't for her; it was only for people with money.

Maya was employed and married with two children. She was a homeowner, had pensions, and had recently started investing outside her pension.

Gathering information to create her list of liabilities was easy: she used her credit report, and she was aware of her outstanding overdraft, car loans and credit card balances. Gathering information to create her list of assets took slightly longer, because Maya hadn't been keeping an eye on her pensions. Over the years, she had been auto-enrolled into various workplace pension schemes but she hadn't created an online account with the provider to keep an eye on the value of them.

Once she had compiled her list of assets and liabilities, we worked out her net worth. It was £25,000. This figure was positive because Maya and her husband owned a property that had increased in value by £60,000 since purchase, and at the same time they were paying off the mortgage. However, what this task highlighted to Maya was the full extent of debt she and her husband had, which was negatively impacting their net worth. Their debt came to £50,000, including credit cards and car loan. Seeing it in black and white felt overwhelming and upsetting – a totally understandable reaction.

Doing this task reaffirmed the need for Maya to tackle the outstanding debt, in order to increase her net worth. Once she has paid off these debts, she can use the money to create assets to further increase her net worth and to make lifestyle changes she and her husband want. When I worked with her, a large percentage of her family income was being used to pay off non-mortgage debt, which meant there was little left to spend on family and herself without feeling guilty.

I was able to reassure Maya that there was light at the end of the tunnel: Maya and her husband were fortunate to have steady jobs and comfortable levels of income which I calculated would enable them to pay off their debts in just under three years.

To calculate your net worth, you need two simple pieces of information: all your assets and all your liabilities and/or debts. Your assets are anything you own that is of value, so that might include your property, your car, any cash you have in bank accounts (include savings accounts, pensions and other investment accounts), the value of your business, or any collectable art or jewellery you own. Your liabilities, on the other hand, are anything you owe, such as credit card debt, student loans, outstanding mortgage balance and bank loans.

Once you have your lists, add up the value of all your assets, then do the same for your liabilities. Next, take away your total liabilities from your assets, and this will give you your net worth figure.

Have a go using my net worth calculator:

Net Worth Calculator

Assets	Liabilities
_____	_____
_____	_____
_____	_____
_____	_____
_____	_____
_____	_____
_____	_____
_____	_____
_____	_____
_____	_____
_____	_____
_____	_____

Total asset value	Total liability value
_____	_____

Your net worth

_____

What number did you get? Was it positive or negative? Whatever the figure, it's okay. As I said earlier, now you know your net worth, and this can be your benchmark. Make sure you add today's date to your calculation so that when you recalculate your net worth, whether that's in six months or in a year, you'll have a clear idea of where you started on your financial journey and the progress you've made.

When I calculated my net worth for the first time and added up all my liabilities – my student loan debt, my overdraft and my maxed-out credit card – I was devastated. Seeing the reality written down in black and white was not pretty, but it validated my emotional state around money. It's an understatement to say that I didn't feel great about it; not only did I not confide in anyone about my financial struggles, but I was also ignoring letters from my credit card company and rejecting phone calls from unknown numbers in case it was the bank calling. However, I can see now that – as upsetting as seeing my minus net worth number was – identifying who, and what, I owed spurred me into turning things around.

Now that you have calculated your net worth, what next? If, like it was for me, your net worth is a minus number, I suggest setting yourself a goal of getting out of the red. To do this, you need to focus on paying off your debts and increasing your assets. If your net worth is positive but on the low side, you should focus on minimising spending by cutting your liabilities and increasing your income – maybe by asking for a pay rise at work, or creating business beyond your main nine to five. This could be anything from creating extra income though a side hustle (such as selling artwork) or starting a business (based on your existing skills), or it could be getting a second job, if this doesn't conflict with your current role.

Have a think about your current workplace. Are there any jobs you could apply for that suit your skill set and will increase your earnings? When did you last have a pay rise? Are you being paid in line with the rate for your job? Do some research on this and think about the best time to approach the topic with your manager (beware: if your company is currently making redundancies due to Covid-19, now is not the best time to ask). During recessions salaries tend to stay the same; however, you could spend some time building up a file of evidence and reasons why your boss should consider giving you a pay rise when the business is back on solid ground again.

Write down your goals for your future net worth in the space below. Maybe you want to focus on increasing it by £20,000 over the next five years, or you may want to start a business. You could also pay off outstanding debt. This will help to increase your net worth. Things change; my own net worth has been impacted in the last few years by being on the property ladder and building up equity in properties I own, as well as by my decision to pay off my debts and start to regularly save and invest money.

_____

_____

_____

_____

_____

_____

_____

Make a commitment to check your net worth at least once a year, to ensure it is going in the direction you want. This is important: if you continue to bury your head in the sand, you don't just miss opportunities to improve your financial reality, but you also miss out on the chance to celebrate your progress. I say this from experience. After the first time I calculated my net worth, I was too frightened to check it for a long time but, when I eventually did, I wished I'd checked it sooner, because I would have noticed how much my net worth was increasing, and I could have decided to double down on debt repayments and maximise savings.

For example, take my overdraft debt. I took out an overdraft when I started university. For ten years after leaving university and starting work, I continued to live off my overdraft – without trying to pay it back. Looking back, I realise I should have paid this back sooner to increase my net worth, as I ended up spending a few thousand pounds on overdraft fees over those ten years. My net worth would have increased by £2,600 (which was the amount my overdraft eventually went up to, from £500 at the start) had I addressed it much sooner, and the monthly overdraft fee I was paying (£28) could have been redirected to another investment that would have increased, rather than decreased, my net worth.

So, don't be put off: check your net worth regularly to see where you can speed up the increase. Knowing your net worth means you can focus on increasing it. Go on! You can commit to facing your financial reality – and changing it for the better.

4

YOUR CREDIT SCORE

Just like knowing your net worth, finding out your credit score will provide a benchmark from which you can improve. A credit score is really important when it comes to applying for a mortgage to buy a house, so you need to know your score and credit history.

Your credit score, put simply, is a number that reflects the likelihood of you paying back the credit you have been lent – usually by a financial institution, such as a bank. It's a measure of your creditworthiness, or the level of risk you pose to an organisation, so they can tell how good you are at paying back any money you borrow. The higher your credit score, the better the chance of you being accepted when you apply for credit. A good credit score also means you are likely to be offered a favourable interest rate on any credit offered, because you present less risk to that lender. On the other hand, the lower your credit score, the higher the risk you are deemed to present to a lending organisation. This can mean that, when you apply for credit, you may be declined or, if your credit application is accepted, it may come with a higher interest rate.

Another thing to be aware of is that a lender's risk appetite can change: sometimes the products they offer reflect the fact that their appetite for risk has increased, whereas at other times it will indicate they have a low-risk appetite. As an illustration, at the start of the Covid-19 pandemic there was a large number of higher loan-to-value (LTV) mortgage products for first-time buyers to choose from (these increase the risk for the lender), whereas once we were in lockdown, the number of higher-risk LTV products on offer reduced considerably. This move towards lower-risk offers was made to protect banks during this period of uncertainty.

Anyway, it's worth knowing your credit score, so you can improve your chance of being able to borrow credit at the best deal (i.e. the lowest interest rate).

Hard and soft credit searches

It's important to be aware of the difference between hard and soft credit searches. You should try to avoid activity that will result in hard searches unless it is absolutely necessary, as they stay on your credit report for twelve months. A hard search is conducted by a lender when you apply for a mortgage, loan or credit card. The lender will take a thorough look at your credit score and decide whether or not to lend you money or allow you to open an account with them. One way to avoid a hard search is to use an eligibility checker, which can carry out soft searches. A soft search is a preliminary credit check, which will give a lender some information about you without looking at your full report. The crucial difference between them is that soft searches are not recorded on your credit report, but hard searches are. Soft searches will also let you know your chance of being accepted before you apply for a financial product such as a loan, and using them can help reduce the risk of rejections damaging your credit score.*

---

* This website explains hard and soft searches more fully: https://www.checkmyfile.com/articles/what-credit-checks-look-for-when-you-switch-energy.htm

So, how do you find out your credit score? Well, credit scores are calculated by credit reference agencies, and they calculate your credit score by reviewing your credit history. The three main agencies in the UK are Equifax, Experian and TransUnion (which used to be called Callcredit), and they gain information about your financial history by collecting data from the organisations you borrow from and do business with. Lenders will regularly report to these agencies about whether you make payments on time or have ever defaulted, and they also pull through information from public records, such as whether you have been made bankrupt or have county court judgements (I'll explain what they are later in this chapter) against you. So, whenever you apply to a lender for credit, that lender has a right to access your credit report and decide, based on that information, whether they want to lend to you. This information is stored on your credit report for six years, so it's worth making sure it's as good as it can be. That's why I want you to look at your credit score today, right now.

Finding out your credit score

You can access your credit score by signing up to one of the above agencies via their website. They usually provide a thirty-day free trial period, followed by a rolling monthly fee that can be cancelled at any time. There are also some smaller companies that provide free access, but their reports tend not to be as detailed as those by the larger agencies. Lenders get their reports from the main agencies, so you should ensure that you're looking at the same information as them.

If you have already checked your credit score with more than one company, you will know that each company uses different credit scores. Here's a breakdown of the credit score ranges for the main agencies:

Experian: 0–999
Equifax: 300–850
TransUnion: 0–710

Alongside your number, they will usually display a description of how you are doing:

Very poor

Poor

Fair

Good

Excellent

Confusingly, credit reference agencies use different scoring methods to calculate your credit score; no one beyond these companies really knows why. That means your request for credit may be denied and it may not be immediately clear why – but I'm going to tell you some handy ways of keeping score yourself.

Let's say you currently utilise a large amount of credit – maybe you already have numerous credit cards and these are all maxed out. When you apply for another credit card or loan, the new lender might worry that, if you get into financial trouble, since you're already committed to paying back a lot of credit, you wouldn't manage to pay back a new line of credit. A big factor that lenders look at is your credit utilisation ratio, which can account for up to 30% of your credit score. Lenders work out how much credit you have available in total and the percentage you are using. If you are regularly utilising over 30% of the credit available to you, this may suggest you are struggling with cash flow and not managing your debts well – even if this is not the case.

Don't be hard on yourself if your credit score is on the low side or not where you want it to be. My credit score was poor when I first checked it. I opened my first bank account when I was in secondary school, after an adviser from Lloyds TSB gave a talk at my school. It stayed more or less dormant and empty until I got my first job – but even before I started my career, I'd been to university and racked up student loan debt (in my head, this was free money every few months). I'd also taken out a bank overdraft simply because a leaflet told me to, to manage my living costs at university. I quickly became overdrawn, and this only increased over the following years. It crept up constantly until I couldn't borrow any more money and I stayed overdrawn for a decade. I look back at this time of racking up debt and recall feeling weirdly validated, as though I was adulting whenever I applied for credit and was accepted. I thought this was what grown-ups did. You applied for a student loan, an overdraft to cover costs, credit cards and eventually a mortgage: congratulations, you're an adult with secret debt (and it's a secret because, remember, you're not allowed to talk about money).

Take it from me, finding out your credit score is the

first thing you need to do to improve it. Obviously, whatever you do, try your best not to miss any payments, but remember that your credit score, just like your net worth, can be improved. There is a myth that, once you get a black mark on your score, you will be blacklisted and never allowed to borrow money again. It's true that you may not be able to get the best interest rates from lenders, but if you have better money management skills, you can begin to make choices that will improve your score. There is still hope – don't give up! Plus, items such as missed payments and defaults drop off your report over time, so anything negative won't stay there forever. In the meantime, you can start building up your score.

To get started, make a note of your credit score below (the number and description) and don't forget to date it. When you come back to this book and look at this page in the future, I want you to look back and see exactly how much your credit score has improved – and how far you have come.

Score: _____

Description: _____

Date: _____

In future, you will be able to look back at your credit score and understand how it changed when you took certain actions. I like scrolling back through my history, as I find it interesting to see how my credit score has changed. However, your credit score won't change immediately; it can take weeks before it reflects a change you have made.

Now you've found out your credit score and noted it here, it's time to take steps to improve it. Here are some basic things to keep in mind when trying to improve your credit score.

Use your credit card sensibly

Banks want to know that you can borrow a reasonable amount of money and pay it back on time. So, don't max out your spending limit (the sweet spot is between 10% and 30% of your credit card limit).

Don't make several applications for credit in a short period of time

Every time you apply for credit, regardless of whether it is accepted or declined, a lender will leave a mark on your credit report, which is visible to credit agencies. If there are multiple marks in a short space of time, it can look as though you are desperate for credit, and they may assume you are in financial difficulty.

Any application for credit needs to be considered and planned in advance, as applying for extra credit can have the effect of increasing your utilisation ratio, thereby lowering your credit score. If you want to apply for a mortgage in the near future, it's a good idea to avoid applying for credit for smaller, unimportant things, such as a new mobile phone contract, within three to six months of you wanting to apply for a mortgage. The number of lines of credit you've recently opened accounts for 10% of your credit score.

Try not to change address too many times in a short period

Banks and other lenders want to lend money to people who are stable. They want to confirm that you are who you say you are, so they will carry out checks (e.g. checking you are on the electoral roll) to verify who you are and where you live, to reduce the risk of fraud. Multiple changes of address can indicate less stability – and an increased risk of fraudulent activity.

Keep your personal information up to date

Mistakes such as errors in your name or address can give a false reflection of your credit history and result in you not benefiting from your diligent work in managing your money. You want to ensure that when you apply for credit you are being assessed on accurate information about you and your financial history.

Most credit report apps and websites have a help section where you can reach out to an expert and ask a question about your report or point out errors on your report. If the error has been added by a third party (e.g. a bank), then contact the third party to say that you are disputing the issue and would like the error to be changed. You may need to follow their complaints procedure if the error is not immediately resolved.

If it can't be fixed, you can add a notice of correction to your report. This is a 200-word statement explaining why a debt is showing on your report, and why this is not a true reflection of how you usually meet repayments.

Try not to miss payments or make too many late payments

Your payment history is recorded on your credit report, and even one missed payment can impact your score. It's important for lenders to be able to ensure you will pay back any borrowed credit, so your payment history and any missed payments accounts for 35% of your credit score. Missed and late payments can result in defaults being added to your report. A default means that the lender has decided that, by missing payments, you have broken your side of the agreement you signed, and they now consider the agreement cancelled – and with their collections department. Each lender is different: some will only allow you to miss or delay one payment before applying a default, whereas others may wait three months before applying a default. Lenders need to follow certain processes in terms of contacting you to ask for repayment and notifying you that a default will be applied.

County court judgements

If you fail to pay a debt to a lender, they can apply for a county court judgement against you to get you to pay the money back. These are kept on the public record so will be seen by lenders. Information that is available in public records – such as being on the electoral roll, county court judgements, individual voluntary arrangements and bankruptcies – will all show on your report and will be visible to lenders.

Bankruptcy

You can apply for bankruptcy if you are struggling to pay off debts. Someone you owe money to (a creditor) can ask a court to make you bankrupt against your will (but they can only do this if you owe £5,000 or more). A bankruptcy is shown on public records, so if you are made bankrupt, a lender will see this.

Individual voluntary arrangements

An individual voluntary arrangement (IVA) is a formal legal agreement between yourself and your creditors. It is arranged through a qualified professional called an insolvency practitioner or an accountant. The practitioner will deal with your creditors on your behalf for the duration of your agreement (usually five to six years). If, by the time the agreement ends, you have not finished paying off all your debt, you do not need to repay the rest. You pay the agreed amount to the insolvency practitioner and they distribute this money to your creditors – and take their fee. It is important to note that there are some restrictions to what debt can be included here: mortgage and rent payments cannot usually be included, and the fee to set up an IVA is usually high, so if your debts total less than £10,000, then this option is probably not right for you.

Missing and default payments will be marked on your credit report for six years – longer in the case of bankruptcy. Imagine yourself in six years' time: think how disappointed you'd be if your application for credit was declined or if you had to settle for a lender who charged an enormous rate of interest due to a missed phone bill payment over five years ago. These factors indicate to a lender that you have got into serious financial difficulty in the past, and they often hold the most weight when calculating your credit score.

Here are some other factors to bear in mind. Your credit history length can account for 15% of your credit score. This means lenders will review how long you've had a bank account to get an insight into your trustworthiness – for example, if you have had the same account with a lender for years, this can indicate to a new lender that you have been able to successfully meet your obligations. Lastly, your credit mix can account for 10% of your credit score. A lender will look at the mixture of credit sources you have available to you (e.g. to see if you have a mixture of revolving credit and other loan types). Having a mixture of credit – such as credit cards, a car loan and a mortgage – can be a bonus, as lenders like to see that you can handle various types of credit responsibly.

Now that you know what your credit score is and have more of an understanding of the factors that impact your score, think about what you can do to improve it. For example, perhaps you could make sure you're on the electoral roll in your area. If you're thinking of applying for a credit card, you may choose to conduct an eligibility search first to ensure no unnecessary hard searches appear on your credit report. You might decide to check your credit utilisation – is it over 30%? If so, try to get it below 30%.

CASE STUDY: CREDIT SCORE

Client: Rhea

Rhea arranged a session with me to sort out some problems she was having with her previous bank and a default that had been added to her credit report.

Rhea's bank account had been unexpectedly closed by her bank. When we spoke first, Rhea told me she hadn't been able to find out why this had happened. (This is not uncommon; banks don't have to tell you why your account has been closed.) She was also struggling to open a new high-street bank account which – I'm sure you can imagine – was a nightmare. She had spent several weeks being given incorrect information by the bank and had to go into the branch to get her wages back, because Rhea's access to her account, and payments, had been frozen. I can only imagine the stress Rhea felt at having to rearrange direct debits and incoming funds, such as her wages. The whole experience was dispiriting and stressful. Imagine one day being able to access your account and your money, and the next day not having any access.

Fortunately, Rhea had managed to open an account with a new online bank. Because she had been refused a standard bank account with another high-street bank, I suggested to Rhea that she started by looking at her credit report. If you are refused credit or can't open an account, always start there: you need to understand what is on your credit report. When she checked, she found that a default had been added to her report by her previous bank. This also meant that her credit score was poor.

We decided on a two-pronged approach: first, she would formally complain to her previous bank about the lack of assistance they had given her when they decided to close her account, and ask for the default on her credit report to be removed. Second, Rhea would improve her credit score (this is not something that will happen immediately). There were two problems: the default on the account and low credit utilisation. Rhea had not used much credit (she had no credit cards, she had no overdraft facility). She was also not on the electoral roll.

At present, Rhea is going through the bank's internal complaints process, and has decided to take her complaint to the Financial Ombudsman Service. We are waiting for the outcome of the complaint. We have also considered the pros and cons of using a credit (re)build card. And she has ensured that she is now on the electoral roll.

Since Rhea came to me, her credit rating has been increased to 'fair', which shows that time can help. It also helps if you are on the electoral roll. The reason her credit score is important

> to Rhea is because she wants to get on the property ladder in the future.
>
> I have included this case study because it illustrates the importance of being aware of what is on your credit report and immediately disputing any errors. Also, do not hesitate to take your case to the Financial Ombudsman Service: it's free to do this, and may help to rectify your score if a genuine error has been made. Banks have a duty to treat customers fairly and to rectify any errors they have made.

Here are my top tips for keeping your credit score squeaky clean:

- Make sure you keep up to date with *all* payments.
- Keep your credit utilisation below 30%. To work out your utilisation of revolving credit (i.e. credit cards, overdrafts, store credit cards), add up the total credit you have spent across all sources, then divide this number by your total available credit. Then multiply by 100 to get the percentage you are using.
- Remember the benefit of keeping older bank accounts open (but do bear in mind that you need to keep up repayments on these, and the 30% credit utilisation).

- Think about your credit mix. While I don't wish to encourage you to take out any extra credit unnecessarily – particularly if you have had difficulty managing repayments in the past (like I did), or if it will mean that your finances are stretched or you will be tempted to overspend – adding a new type of credit and managing it properly can help to improve your credit score. Again, bear in mind the 30% utilisation rule, and be mindful of the number of new accounts you apply for in a short time.

So, now that you know how credit scores work and know the steps you need to take to improve yours, it's time to start mapping out your financial goals.

5

TACKLING DEBT

It's time to tackle one of the scariest yet most important aspects of money management. Take a breath and remember all the money mindset lessons we talked about in Chapter 1, because now we're going to talk about debt. Listen, I know that talking about debt is really hard. It can keep you awake at night, particularly if the debt you have to pay back seems like an insurmountable sum. Perhaps your finances are already stretched, or maybe you've spent the past few months or weeks burying your head in the sand. I know what that's like. Being in debt can create feelings of intense shame, anxiety and stress. It's no fun at all, so let's take this chapter easy. I'm with you every step of the way.

One of the first calls I received after I launched Black Girl Finance was from a woman in floods of tears, overwhelmed by her debt. It can't have been easy to make that phone call and open up to me about struggling with debt, especially as she had been unable to discuss it with her friends and family. Her story really affected me because, as you know, my own experience of debt was similarly overwhelming and lonely. One of the main reasons I created Black Girl Finance was to help other women who were in the same situation I had been. I look back at being in debt, too embarrassed to speak to even my twin sister about it. I felt like I had failed.

The first thing I want you to recognise is, **you're not alone**. So many of us fall on hard times, and a mind-bogglingly huge number of people in the UK are in debt. In 2020, 4.6 million British citizens collectively owed at least £6 billion in private debt, and more than one in eight people who have been furloughed had defaulted on a payment.* The pandemic has been cruel to everyone, but it's worth noting that a report published by the Fawcett Society† found that BAME women were more likely to feel forced into debt and be worried about covering basic living costs.

---

* https://www.theguardian.com/commentisfree/2020/aug/05/uk-private-debt-crisis-recession-coronavirus
† https://www.fawcettsociety.org.uk/coronavirus-impact-on-bame-women

This demonstrates how deep structural inequality can be. While we have a lot to be angry about, please remember that you're not alone, and that getting into debt doesn't reflect badly on you as a person. The second thing I want you to know is that it is possible to get out of debt, and your current circumstances do not have to be your future reality.

It's important to tackle debt, because prioritising paying it off makes real, data-driven, number-crunching sense. When you look at how much interest is charged on debt compared to how much interest is paid out on savings and even on investments, getting on top of debt is a no-brainer. The average credit card interest rate is around 20%, whereas the average savings account interest rate is 0.05%. How does this translate to actual money? Well, if you have £1,000 of debt with an annual interest rate of 20%, you will end up paying £200 in interest for the year. If you put that same £1,000 in a savings account, you will end up earning interest of 50p. So you're better off prioritising paying off your debt rather than saving money.

Often, we put off tackling our debt because we don't have a clear debt repayment strategy in mind. That's how it was for me, anyway. When I first got into debt, I had no idea how I'd pay it off. Don't get me wrong; I didn't plan to max out my credit card or regularly increase my credit limit. I just told myself I would use only a little bit each month then pay it back straight away. This happened at first, but gradually, over a number of months, I fell into the trap of spending more money than I had on my credit card – particularly when I was out with friends and wanted to be generous by paying for drinks, or if I was feeling down or bored and ended up going shopping. The temptation to spend was so high that I lost control and was only able to make minimum payments for a while, before panicking and making no payments at all. I tuned out and hit rock bottom.

So, if you're like I was, please don't worry. It's possible to get things back on track. We all need a wake-up call sometimes, and once you hit the bottom there's only one way to go. That's why I'm going to explain two clear strategies for paying off debt. It's never too late! Before I get into the different repayment strategies, I should say that if your debts are so high that you are in danger of losing your home or you have bailiffs visiting, seek urgent, free advice from agencies such as the Money Advice Service or Citizens Advice, which can provide the guidance you need. Also, in this current period of economic uncertainty, it's important to know what financial help and support is available to you through government schemes. I've added some links in the 'Helpful websites' section of the book.

As I mentioned at the beginning of this chapter, it can be extremely painful knowing that you accumulated debt what feels like a lifetime ago; now you have to pay it back, but you don't know where to start. That's why you need to start handling your money like the brand-new person you are. You've got plans to achieve, and being dragged down by past debt is not part of the plan. So, let's get to work.

The first thing you will need to do is make a list of your debts, so you know exactly what you owe and to which company. This part should be straightforward, because you should already have listed your liabilities when you calculated your net worth. Make sure you list your debts in order (from the highest to the lowest amount), and include any minimum payments you need to make.

Here's an example of a list of debts:

Car loan:	£10,000
Mastercard:	£5,000
American Express:	£2,000
Barclaycard:	£1,900
Debit card overdraft:	£1,500
Total:	**£20,400**

Now write yours.

_____

_____

_____

_____

_____

_____

Whatever your list looks like, I hope that, at this stage of the book, you're not beating yourself up. What's happened is in the past, and this is your new start.

Next, you need to work out the best strategy for you. There are two schools of thought when it comes to paying off debt, and the best approach for you depends on what motivates you. The first approach, the debt avalanche, allows you to attack your debt by focusing on the largest amount or the amount with the highest interest rate (which makes financial sense, because you will also be getting rid of the high associated costs). If we apply this strategy to the example above, that means tackling the car loan first. This might make the most sense, but it will take longer to pay off and get that first win (at which stage you can give yourself a massive pat on the back), which might make it a less motivating way to approach your debt. It's worth thinking about this, because some of us are less likely to stick with a strategy if it takes a long time to get to that first big win.

The alternative approach, the debt snowball, starts with repaying smaller debts first, so you get a win sooner, which may keep you motivated to stick with the strategy. While both options will help you to repay your debts, think about which approach best suits you and your personality. Before we get into the dos and don'ts of the avalanche and the snowball strategies, it's important that you commit to not using your credit cards, overdrafts, store cards, etc. from this point onwards. There is no point working hard to pay off debt in one area while raking up more debt somewhere else. Okay? Right, let's get into it.

The snowball method

You already know you need to list your debts in order, from the smallest to the largest. Next, you need to work out the minimum monthly payments for all your debts and start paying those amounts. (The exception is if your smallest debt is your overdraft, in which case you should try to pay as much as you possibly can: this is because if you only make the minimum payments, you will only be paying off the interest charges, rather than chipping away at the actual amount you have borrowed.) Do this consistently each month, and if you find yourself with any extra income, use it to pay a bit more off your lowest debt. It doesn't matter how small the amount is – every £5 helps. The goal is to pay towards all debt simultaneously in a manageable way, rather than trying to make over-payments on all debts all at once, overstretching yourself and giving up.

Once you've paid the first debt, stop and acknowl-edge your triumph: you can pay off debt! You are back in control! This will feel great. Give yourself a high five but don't stop there – oh no, you're on a roll. Now, you're going to snowball the money you used to pay off the first debt to pay off the second-smallest debt. In the example above, that would be the Barclaycard debt of £1,900. The money you were paying towards the first debt now goes towards the second debt, in addition to the original min-imum payment you were making towards the second debt. Once the second debt is paid off, you do the same again: snowball this payment and add it to the minimum payment of the third debt, and so on until all debts have been paid.

The avalanche method

Again, start by listing your debts in the order of highest to lowest. In our example above, the highest is the car finance of £10,000, with a minimum repayment of £179 per month. You pay off what you can afford above this amount, i.e. you pay £210 per month instead. Next, just as with the snowball method, you make the minimum payments each month on all your debts except the largest. For the car finance debt, you pay as much as you can over the minimum payment amount each month.

Once you've paid off the car finance debt, you move on to the next highest debt, which would be the £5,000 on Mastercard, which has a monthly minimum repayment of £120. You avalanche and add the amount you repaid towards the car finance to the minimum payment of the Mastercard, which means you pay £210 + £120 = £330 per month towards the Mastercard debt.

As I said before, when I was struggling with debt, I hadn't heard of either of these methods. I winged it, simply making a lump sum payment to whatever debt was most urgent at the time if I happened to earn extra money or if I borrowed from family. It was all very disorganised, which meant that, although the immediate stress and pressure was off because I'd repaid some money, my finances for the coming month were thrown off. I was constantly short somewhere else, so would resort to spending on a credit card or going into my overdraft. This became a revolving cycle of financial chaos. With no emergency fund, budget, or debt repayment strategy, I lived from payday to stressful payday, without making any headway towards paying off my debt. Finally, I set up a repayment plan for my credit card debt: £100 per month for eighteen months, before I made that balloon payment. As for my overdraft, I was able to pay that off once I sold my home.

CASE STUDY: REPAYING DEBT (1)

Client: Ellie

I clearly remember Ellie's first call because she was sobbing down the phone, such was her distress about the debt she was in. She managed to explain that she was already seeking debt advice through Step Change, the debt charity, which was looking into setting up a debt management plan for her. I praised her for taking such a bold and positive step and advised her to stay engaged with their services. I also mentioned that there were other organisations she could speak to, such as Citizens Advice.

I have included this case study to show that it's okay to seek advice – particularly at this time, with the Covid-19-related job uncertainty and redundancies. Everyone should feel free to explore all options without feeling embarrassed. No one will judge you for getting into debt. However, there are ways to get out of debt, and organisations to help. Which takes me on to my next case study, where I helped Yinka to devise a clear strategy.

CASE STUDY: REPAYING DEBT (2)

Client: Yinka

Yinka had got in touch due to her mounting debt. She was not yet at a stage where she was unable to pay her essential bills, but her finances were stretched and she was painfully aware that it was time to get to grips with her debt. It was almost £6,000, and she lacked a strategy to repay it.

I worked with her to figure out the best strategy. During our call we discussed the pros and cons of the debt snowball and the debt avalanche strategies. She chose the debt snowball to start with, to get some quick wins under her belt, and said she would move on to the avalanche method after some time.

A year after our initial call, Yinka has managed to pay off half her debt. She is on track to pay off the remainder in the next twelve months. All she needed was a clear strategy to follow, and I'm happy I could provide this for her.

I know several women who have paid off significant amounts of debt using one of these methods – in fact, a podcast guest of mine paid off £36,000 of debt using the snowball method. They are tried-and-tested strategies, and they work. I've included both methods, so you can choose which suits you best. Whatever you do, pick a method – and start.

Does it take time? Yes.

Does it take patience? Yes.

Does it take focus? Yes.

Does it take commitment? Yes.

Is it worth it? 100% yes.

I cannot stress enough how important it is to have a clear debt repayment strategy. Most of the time we talk about paying off debt simply by making repayments, without looking at the method behind it. Maybe you agree a repayment of what you can afford with your creditor, without considering the knock-on effect on your other debts or whether this will mean you need to rack up debt elsewhere. I understand these decisions are often made in a knee-jerk way while under pressure; you want to do something to get rid of your debt fast, but this may not give the best results.

With the methods outlined in this chapter, you will be able to relax, knowing that you are still making minimum repayments, so your debts aren't increasing and your creditors will be satisfied. Another benefit is, when you put in all this hard work, you won't want to sabotage your efforts by reverting to your old spending habits. Even if there is a time when you need to leverage some form of credit, in future you will have a clear strategy to pay off any debt.

The goal is to make real strides towards increasing your net worth. Every day you're in debt means money being directed out of your pocket. I'm not saying you shouldn't get on the property ladder using a mortgage, or take out a student loan to study, or get a business loan (if I said this, I'd be a hypocrite!), but I would make it a priority to pay off any debts that have a high interest rate as quickly as possible. Having a debt repayment strategy built into your monthly budget is gold-standard money management, so look at ways in which you can reduce your spending in certain areas and commit to prioritising your debt repayment. I can't emphasise enough how proud of yourself you will be.

6

FINANCIAL GOALS

Before I get started on this chapter, I just want to say well done. Seriously. The last few chapters have required you to take a long, hard look at your financial reality, and that's tough. Doing a deep dive into your money mindset and money management skills is not always comfortable, but I promise you, you will thank yourself for getting through it. Now you have your current financial situation written down, you will be able to look back and see just how far you've come on your financial journey. So, pause, collect your breath and congratulate yourself: I'm proud of your progress, and you should be too.

Now, back to business. Once you've worked out where you are financially, it's time to set some financial goals. Financial goals are an often neglected part of personal development. It is perfectly acceptable for us to have plans for many parts of our lives, such as our career, marriage, travel, family and even things like fitness and skincare, so why don't we have plans for our finances? All of the above areas are important, but why do we leave money to the bottom of the pile? It's absolutely bonkers that so many of us don't prioritise our finances, considering the impact that a lack of financial planning can have on our lives, especially as we get older and are no longer able to work. That's why I urge you to prioritise financial planning.

My lack of money management skills left me struggling financially while I was raising a young child, and it also meant that I made no preparations for my financial future. On the surface, it looked like I was doing well – I had managed to get on the property ladder and was working full-time – but I was paddling furiously to keep myself financially afloat. So, where was I going wrong? I can tell you exactly where: apart from paying my bills, managing my finances was not on my radar. I was not budgeting, I had no emergency fund, I had zero investments and was making minimal pension contributions. I wasn't even thinking about the future, just about what was happening right now. I was going from payday to the next panicked payday. I'd lost track of my credit score (and didn't know the factors that affected it) and I'd never thought about my net worth.

If you write down a goal, you're 42% more likely to achieve it.* So – you guessed it – the first step is to write down your goals. Make them really specific: if you have checked your credit score and want to increase it, your goal should be 'to increase my credit score by 40 points', for example. List your goals below:

_____

_____

_____

_____

_____

_____

_____

_____

_____

_____

* https://www.inc.com/peter-economy/this-is-way-you-need-to-write-down-your-goals-for-faster-success.html

Next, you need to set a realistic time frame to achieve your goals. Whenever I have a financial goal, I write it down clearly and concisely, and I decide on a deadline to meet the goal by. Then I decide on an appropriate step I can take within the week (or even by the next day) and add it to the calendar on my phone (and ensure I switch on alerts!). Let's say your goal is similar to the example above and you want to increase your credit score. Credit score apps are usually extremely good at clearly telling you what to do to improve your score. Some, such as Experian, even give a time frame. This could be anything from three months to a year, which is all well and good, but what immediate steps can you take? Well, once you've checked your score on the app, make a list of the steps you can take to improve it. What factor can you work on first? Let's say the app has flagged up the fact that you aren't on the electoral roll. Your first step? Get on the electoral roll first thing tomorrow. Break each goal down into clear actionable steps, with a time allocated for each one.

This strategy worked for me when I decided to improve my credit score for the second time (the first time was six months before I wanted to get on the property ladder as a first-time buyer). The second time, I was motivated by wanting to improve my financial well-being. I was tired of ignoring phone calls and letters in case they were from creditors. I knew there were things I needed to work on, and I hadn't focused on my credit score since getting on the property ladder. To turn things around, I prioritised paying off debts. To achieve this, I did two things: (1) I cut back my spending by choosing to commute into work using the bus instead of the trains, and I used the money I was saving to pay back some of my debt; (2) I took a bold step and asked for a pay rise at work – and I got it. When I started the process, I felt like I couldn't get out of the financial black hole I was in, but once I got past the feeling of disappointment and got to work, I couldn't believe the difference it made.

CASE STUDY: FINANCIAL GOALS

Client: Samara

I speak to a lot of college and university students who are coming towards the end of their degrees. Samara, a student in the final year of her course, who is also a mum, reached out to me via Instagram and arranged a call. She had financial goals, one of which was getting on the property ladder.

We spoke about what she wanted to do after university, which was to get a job related to her degree. She had already researched opportunities and salaries and was confident that, once she graduated, she would get a job in her chosen field.

When we spoke, we focused on the steps she could take immediately to ensure that she stayed on track for her goal of owning a property. We discussed the process of buying a property: the need for a good credit score, how she planned to raise her deposit, solicitors' fees and all the other costs. Samara lived in local authority accommodation, and had already thought about exploring the right-to-buy scheme. She had also already started saving into a Help to Buy Individual Savings Account (ISA).

After our first call, we spoke regularly. When we spoke three months later, she felt she was closer to her financial goal, which she felt was attainable. She had decided to repay her overdraft, so her credit utilisation was less than 30%. She was also keeping an eye out for available mortgage deals. She was laser-focused on her financial goal.

Often we look at our financial situation in isolation – maybe we want to repay a debt or save for a house deposit – but unless we keep a tally of our financial circumstances, we won't understand how they impact our overall financial goals. You may find that you're spending a lot of time moving the needle in one area, but this might not have the impact you want. For example, if you have high-interest debts that are costing you more than any interest you're earning on your savings, it would be better to tackle the debt first before you focus on saving. That way, you can increase your net worth. That's why it's good to keep track of your credit score, net worth and budget, because this enables you to track the great progress you're making and spot areas where you can improve. So, set yourself those calendar reminders.

Have a think about what goals will really change your situation – not just in the next year, but also in the next five years and beyond – and jot down your thoughts in the planner below. Here are some suggestions for things you might include:

- Short term: this box is for goals that can be accomplished within the next six months to a year, such as identifying ways to increase your credit score, contacting creditors about debts, or creating and implementing a budget strategy.
- Mid term: this section is for goals that will take between one to five years. Examples might include saving for a deposit to buy your first home, starting your own business, or putting money aside for your wedding.
- Long term: this is for goals that will take more than five years to achieve, such as investing in long-term shares, contributing money to your pension fund, or significantly increasing your net worth.

Goals

Short term	Action/Date

Mid term	Action/Date

Long term	Action/Date

We've already addressed ways you can work on your short-term financial goals, so the next few chapters explain how you can grapple with your bigger goals. First up is saving for those rainy days.

7

SAVING

It doesn't take a genius to realise that the earlier you start saving, the larger the rewards and benefits you will reap, but research has found that a quarter of British adults have no savings whatsoever.* Saving has become even harder for many of us due to the Covid-19 pandemic and the devastating job losses it has caused. This has disproportionately impacted BAME workers, with around 15% reporting losing their jobs compared to an estimated 8% of white workers,† and women being one-third more

---

* https://www.independent.co.uk/news/uk/home-news/
british-adults-savings-none-quarter-debt-cost-living-emergencies-
survey-results-a8265111.html
† https://www.independent.co.uk/news/uk/politics/coronavirus-
economic-effect-uk-ethnic-minorities-young-people-a9460511.html

likely to work in a sector that is currently affected (such as retail, hospitality and travel) than men.* This means it's more important than ever for Black women to get into the habit of saving to protect themselves against misfortune.

A lack of savings translates directly to pension poverty, and the risk of finding yourself in this dire situation is increased massively if you are Black or from an ethnic minority background. In 2019, Age UK identified that 33% of Asian British pensioners and 30% of Black pensioners live in poverty, compared to just 15% of white pensioners. The rate of pension poverty increases again if you're female, and even more if you're single.†

At the time of writing, the current full UK state pension is £175.20 per week (or £9,110.40 per year). Let's face it, this is not a lot of money to live on (and there's no guarantee that state pensions will even be available in the next thirty or forty years). Think about your current expenses; the state pension is probably a lot less than your current weekly expenses. While many employees are automatically

---

* https://commonslibrary.parliament.uk/research-briefings/cbp-8898
† Age UK, 'Poverty in later life: a briefing' (2020).

enrolled on their employers' pension schemes (you can opt out, but that's generally not a good idea due to the many benefits you receive, such as employer contributions and tax breaks), the amount put into employee pension schemes might not be enough for you to live on in future. If you're self-employed or working in the gig economy, the onus is on you to save and start a pension. (The gig economy is a way of working where people engage in one-off jobs and are paid per job, or gig, rather than working for an employer. Consumers are connected to people able to carry out the job via a marketplace, such as the Uber app or fiverr.com.)

I'm not saying any of this to scare you, but to help you realise that relying on the state pension as your sole source of future income is not wise. So, what can you do? First, you need to start picturing the lifestyle you want at retirement. To do this, ask yourself the following questions:

- How much do I currently earn each month?
- Will I need the same monthly amount to maintain the lifestyle I want in retirement?
- How much does that lifestyle cost now? (Add inflation, because the cost of living only goes in one direction, which is up!)

- Do I want to remain in the UK or move
  abroad? If you want to move, where do you
  want to go?

We all have different financial needs, so it's a good idea to start planning your pension as soon as possible. Work out how much you need to save to afford the lifestyle you want. Remember that any inheritance tax (IHT) that your family has to pay upon your death is calculated by balancing your assets and liabilities. However, not everyone has to pay IHT, as there is a threshold; as of 2020, IHT is only payable on houses worth over £325,000.*

It may be horrible to think about, but it's better to be prepared and to have these conversations with your loved ones now, so that they know your wishes. To ensure that your assets are protected, you need to take professional advice from a qualified financial adviser.

Anyway, back to the land of the living. You should speak to a qualified financial adviser about your pension options, and there are a number of free pension calculators available online (I've included a list in the 'Helpful

---

* See https://www.gov.uk/browse/tax/inheritance-tax for more on all aspects of inheritance tax.

websites' section at the back of the book). These allow you to type in how much money you wish to have per year upon retirement and work out how much you need to save each year to achieve this. Doing this can help you decide whether to increase your contributions or postpone retiring for a few years so you have more time to build up your pension pot.

I had zero clue about pensions when I first started working, which was back before auto-enrolment* came into effect and before I chose to get better at handling money (it *is* a choice). Even though I was working full-time and progressing in my career, a pension felt like something for older people. I'd received informative emails and had been invited to presentations hosted by the HR department about the employee pension scheme, but I didn't really engage with them until I decided to take a closer look at my pension. After I'd set up an online account with my pension provider (this took me months) and looked into how much pension

---

* Auto-enrolment is a government initiative to get employees saving for their financial futures through their workplace pension. Previously the onus was on the employee to join the workplace pension scheme. Now, under auto-enrolment, employees are automatically put into their workplace pension scheme – though they can still choose to opt out.

I had saved, I was gobsmacked by how little it was. It was no more than a few hundred pounds – barely enough to do a monthly food shop, let alone enough to retire on. You can imagine how stressed I was. Fast-forward a few years and my pension pot is looking a lot healthier. But I know that if I'm lucky enough to live for thirty years after I retire, those thousands won't be enough to survive on. So I have to ramp up my contributions. That's the moral of the story: pay attention to your pension. How much is in your pot? Is it enough?

I'm glad I started to take my pension fund seriously and increased my contributions. The key to successful pension planning is to start early: the sooner you start saving, the smaller your monthly payments need to be. Starting early also allows time for the power of compound interest (something I'll explain in Chapter 9) to take effect. It helped me to think of my pension as a gift to my future self. Paying into a pension might mean sacrificing some things now, but you will reap the benefits later. There's truly no better insurance.

If you have the funds, you can open a Self-Invested Personal Pension (SIPP) for anyone, including your children. You can add up to £2,880 per child per year, which attracts tax relief of £720 per year, totalling £3,600. Once they turn eighteen, they can take over managing their account, but they will not be able to access their pension until they're fifty-five (this is true at the time of writing this book; however, the government has announced that this will change in future).

Apart from setting money aside, you can also invest in property, with the idea of selling it later on to release equity or supplementing your pension with rental income. You might also consider putting some money in an ISA; although you do not get the same upfront tax benefits with ISAs as you do with pensions, they are a tax-efficient wraparound, which means your investments are shielded from some or all taxes. If, for example, you set up an investment ISA and purchased all your shares through it, you will not be taxed on any interest you earn, dividends* you receive, or any increase in the value of the shares.

---

* A dividend is a sum of money paid regularly (typically, annually) by a company to its shareholders out of its profits (or reserves).

CASE STUDY: SAVINGS

Client: Leila

Leila, who had stopped work due to ill-health, decided to speak to me about savings, because she felt she needed to get her finances back on track. She felt stressed and trapped in a negative cycle.

In our first call, Leila described herself as having a bad relationship with money. She had got used to not having any money left each month after her income had come in and she had paid all her expenses and debts. She was also receiving letters and phone calls from debt collectors chasing money she owed for online shopping.

I spoke to Leila about how important it was to set up her environment so she was not tempted to spend: she could do this by unsubscribing to emails from retailers, so she wasn't constantly shown tempting items to buy. The second thing we spoke about was the importance of getting into the mindset that, when she received her benefits, she paid herself first (by regularly saving a percentage of her income).

She also needed to regain control of her repayments to her creditors, so she had to budget.

When I spoke to Leila again, she had taken steps such as unsubscribing from tempting email lists. She had also opened a separate savings account and set up a standing order so that each month money automatically went into her savings account. She explained that now she felt empowered and in total control of her money. Rather than having zero money left over each month, she could see her savings building up, and she was recently able to increase her monthly savings because she had cleared her debts.

She told me she no longer felt stressed and punished for not having money. She felt she could plan for her future. Leila was back in control.

Use the pension planner below to document your pensions and savings for the long term. Note down the amount you want to have saved for retirement along with any additional ideas, such as investing in property and personal savings. Also consider how many years you have left to save until you reach your desired retirement age.

Pension providers
(names and phone numbers)

Amount in each pension

Pensions
Plan

Goal amount

Monthly saving

Again, you should refer back to your plan regularly to ensure you're saving enough and that your plan is on track. Review it once a year. Make sure, if you do change jobs, that you don't lose track of your pension. If you need to track old pensions, use the free pensions tracing service (listed in the 'Helpful websites' section at the back of the book).

Saving for later life is really important and should be incorporated into your monthly budget. Saving for your pension means investing in your future self. I don't have a crystal ball, so – annoyingly – I can't predict how much the UK state pension will be in the future, or how long we'll live after retirement, but it's still worth looking into. You can't afford to let your future self down.

8

BUILDING AN
EMERGENCY FUND

Okay, so you know it's important to save for your future retirement, but what about putting aside some money for the here and now? There will be times when you'll need money unexpectedly – for example, to buy a new boiler or to replace your car. So often my clients say they have no savings to deal with an emergency. During a workshop I hosted recently, one participant said she'd travelled abroad and had got stranded, with no money to travel back. She had to rely on the kindness of relatives to get back home. Another spoke of a family emergency abroad; she had been unable to afford to get there because she was paying off debts. During the workshops we get really comfortable and candid when talking about money, and hearing frequent conversations about clients not having money to deal with an emergency prompted me to write this chapter.

In life, things happen at random. You never know when you may have a water leak or an unexpected bill to pay. That's why building up an emergency fund is a key component of good money management.

Research conducted by the World Economic Forum* found that women save less than men each month. While this is no doubt due to the GPG, it doesn't change the fact that it is super important that we start saving our pounds and pennies. If we have money saved up for an emergency, we don't have to get into more debt if the worst happens. I know it's not easy, but it's worthwhile building up an emergency pot. And no, before you ask – a credit card is not an emergency fund! Nice try, though.

An emergency fund is a pot of money made up of three to six months' worth of living expenses. It is only to be used in emergencies. It should be kept separate from savings earmarked for short- or long-term plans: resist the temptation to use it for everyday spending! Most importantly, it needs to be liquid (i.e. easily accessible).

---

* https://www.weforum.org/agenda/2018/03/retired-women-less-money-pensions-than-men

Whenever you take money from the fund, you need to build it back up as soon as possible. Having an emergency fund is an essential part of a money management plan.

The importance of having an emergency fund cannot be underestimated. By setting aside this pot of money, you'll be:

1. Less likely to be stressed out in a financial emergency.
2. Less likely to get into unexpected debt.
3. Less likely to dip into money reserved for your other financial goals.

To illustrate the need for an emergency fund, think about the following scenarios. Ashley learns that a family member has died abroad and she needs to get on the next flight to that country to help. It will cost £800 to fly out and contribute to the cost of the funeral.

Bella is driving to work when her car judders to a halt. Once it has been taken to a garage and assessed, Bella is told that it will cost £800 to fix the fault.

Chelsea has an old boiler that has been recently making a weird noise. She gets home from work one day and finds that the boiler won't switch on, which means she no longer has hot water or heating. Shame, as it's the middle of a particularly cold winter. Chelsea calls out a boiler repair man, who tells her the boiler needs to be replaced, and this will cost £800.

None of the women in these scenarios has an emergency fund. Instead, they have money tied up in goal-oriented savings. Ashley intends to pay off debts of £1,000 in the next six months. Bella has a goal of saving £1,000 over the next six months. Chelsea is saving for a deposit towards a property purchase. These emergencies have occurred just after payday, so they feel okay about making the emergency payment. However, Ashley will still have to make her debt repayments as well as pay her monthly household bills. Due to their emergencies, Bella and Chelsea are unable to save towards their goals, which means they are delayed for this month. All will struggle through the month, and potentially beyond.

Now think about these scenarios again, but this time imagine that the emergencies occurred later in the month and the three women have already spent their wages on their living expenses. They might be tempted to take out some form of expensive debt (a payday loan, credit card, bank loan or overdraft) to cover the cost of the emergency, which means it has plunged them into debt and/or delayed their other financial goals.

Finally, imagine the scenarios once more, only this time each woman has £1,000 in an easily accessible emergency fund. Once Ashley has paid for the cost of the flight and the funeral, she can use her salary to continue paying off her original debt, as planned. After dipping into their emergency funds to cover the cost of fixing their car or replacing their boiler, Bella and Chelsea can get closer to their savings goals. As this example illustrates, having an emergency fund allows you to deal with unexpected emergencies with less stress, less debt and greater peace of mind.

Think about a time when *you* have had to pay out money in an emergency. Did you have money available or did you have to take out additional debt? If the latter, don't worry – it's never too late to start.

Let's look at how to create an emergency fund. First, are you telling yourself that you can't save, that you can't afford to save, that extra money is hard to come by, that you struggle with money? Stop right now. These messages are holding you back. Flip the narrative and tell yourself that you can save, that you're good with money, that money flows to you easily and regularly. You can achieve anything you set your mind on. Before you go any further, write a message to yourself below to help you get into a positive money mindset:

_____

_____

_____

Okay, let's proceed. First, open a savings account with your current bank. Keeping a separate savings account means that you're less likely to touch it for anything less than a genuine emergency. If you find you can't resist the temptation to dip into it, I'd recommend opening a new account at a different bank. Having it in a separate account away from the money you use to cover bills, and any other long-term savings account you might have, means it's out of sight – and hopefully out of mind – until an emergency arises. Wherever you keep your emergency fund, make sure it's easily accessible and that you won't be charged for making withdrawals. Make sure it's not in an investment account (what if the value of your investments goes down just as an emergency occurs?). A simple, no-frills account is all you need.

Creating an emergency fund should be part of your money management plan. Every single payday, get into the habit of paying a sum into your emergency fund first – before anything else. While your long-term goal should be to save three to six months' worth of income, saving less than this is perfectly acceptable to start with. If you can only set aside £100 to start with, that's an important first step to creating a financial buffer.

If you don't have any extra cash, think about one unnecessary expense you can live without. I started my savings habit in my thirties by saving £50 each month. To achieve this, I got rid of my £60-per-month gym membership, which I hardly used. I know, I'm a total cliché. But I'm not alone. Research carried out by Fridge Raiders in 2019* found that, in Britain, 23% of people have gym memberships but only 12% reported going to the gym regularly, wasting almost £4 billion annually. Be honest with yourself: if you're not using your membership, it's money you could save or invest elsewhere.

Here are some other ways you could free up money to top up your emergency fund:

---

* https://www.thedailybrit.co.uk/brits-waste-over-369-million-monthly-on-unused-gym-membership

- If you receive a bonus at work, put it into your emergency fund.
- If you get a tax rebate, put it into your emergency fund.
- Sell things you no longer need on a marketplace like eBay, Depop or Shpock.
- Create a side hustle (see below). Sign up to Fiverr, Uber, Deliveroo – do whatever you can to make extra income.

Side hustles

Whatever your financial situation and circumstances, there may come a time when you need to make extra income. Here are some ideas for side hustles that you can do from home and that can fit around your job. All you will need for most is a laptop/tablet plus a headset.

- Virtual assistant – If you're super organised and have the time and skills, being a virtual assistant to help out small businesses could be a great role for you.
- Social media content creator – If you have an eye for design and are great at using editing tools such as Canva

or Photoshop, you could advertise your services to business owners, who will pay you to design templates that they can use across their social media platforms.

- Social media co-ordinator – If you're organised, a good writer, and great at using Instagram, Twitter, Pinterest and so on, you could run social media and marketing campaigns for small businesses.

- Selling on eBay, Facebook Marketplace, Shpock, Vinted, etc. – If you have clothes that your kids have grown out of, or things around the house you no longer need, why not list them on one of the many selling websites?

- Logo designer – Many new and existing businesses need help to create a logo as part of their brand identity. If you have an eye for design, creating new logos or updating old ones could be a service you can offer.

- Website designer – There is high demand for website designers to create websites from scratch or to redesign existing websites.

- Search engine optimisation (SEO) services – Making sure that your company is listed on the first page of Google is super important for businesses. There are many ways to achieve this, including using SEO. If you know how to do this, then you can provide a valuable service to businesses.

- Translating services – If you speak another language fluently, you can use this skill. Many organisations require translators, as do businesses that pair translators to their clients. Search for translation businesses online – they usually have a section where you can sign up as a translator.
- Surveys – Filling in online surveys is a great way to earn small amounts of extra income for giving your opinions on various topics.
- Focus groups – Organisations are always looking for real people to talk to, who are happy to share their thoughts on various topics.
- Online tutoring – If you have qualifications, you could consider online tutoring in subjects as diverse as maths, the sciences, playing the guitar or art.
- YouTube tutorials – I'm sure we all have our favourite YouTubers we follow. If they can do it, why not you? There are rules around monetising YouTube accounts. If you have a big following and enjoy sharing your opinions on issues you're passionate about, and you aren't afraid to be in front of a camera, this is an option.
- Write a blog – If you're a good writer, you could create a blog. If there is a subject you're passionate about, know a lot about, and in an area that is not saturated with

bloggers, there could be ways to monetise your blog through affiliate links, sponsorship and ads.

- Write content for articles – Again, if you love writing and are good at it, there are many online and print publications that will pay for people to create content.
- Podcasting – If you love to talk, you could create a podcast and monetise it through sponsored ads.

Some of the jobs listed above may require additional qualifications and skills. Do your research, explore all options and think about your transferable skills.

Once I had paid off my debts, I started to redirect some of the money I was using to pay back my debt to build up my emergency fund. My emergency fund is kept in a separate bank account, which I have easy access to through an app on my smartphone. It also comes with a debit card, which is useful if I need to make a quick payment. I also used creative ways to top up my emergency fund when it ran low. I won a TV from work once and promptly sold it, and when I won Amazon vouchers, I bought things that I then sold on Shpock or eBay.

The trick here is to be creative and think outside the box. We all have marketable skills. Are you artistic? Look for old pieces of furniture you could upcycle and sell on. (Look on your local Freegle group for people giving away furniture.) Are you a great cook? You could start a supper club (Covid-19 rules permitting). Do you sew? You could offer repairs and alterations, or customise clothing to sell. Could you create an online course based on your skills and teach it?

Once you've set up your emergency fund, you need to decide what constitutes an 'emergency'. Before taking money out of your emergency fund, I suggest you assess the level of the emergency: score it on a scale of 1 to 10 (where 10 is a disaster). Think about whether there is another way to handle this. If it still feels like a level 7–10 emergency, then use the fund. It is designed to act as a safety net, after all.

For Bella in our earlier example, who relied on her car for work, her emergency could be a 7 or 8. Someone who does not rely on their car for work could wait until next month to get it fixed.

Once you've dipped into your emergency fund, you absolutely must top it back up again, using the same method you used to build it. Creating an emergency fund should be factored into your budget. You're simply adding a financial buffer to help you deal with emergencies without denting your future financial well-being. Honestly, try it. You'll thank me later.

CASE STUDY: COVID-19

Client: Shayna

Shayna was one of the first women to book a call with me when I started to offer Black Girl Finance coaching calls.

She felt that her financial situation was out of control. She had debts to pay off and had little in savings. She mentioned that she'd financed her wedding and house moves through credit cards.

Shayna has a decent income each month. When she worked out her budget, she had £430 left over each month after she'd paid all her bills and debts. This allowed her to start building up her emergency fund so she would not have to rely on credit cards. After our call, she decided to work on building up her emergency fund to £1,000, then she aimed for three times her monthly expenses.

Eight months later, the emergency fund she had built up came in handy when she was given notice to move out of her rented accommodation. This was at the start of Covid-19; her landlord had decided to move back into the property. Shayna was able to negotiate with her landlord to move out before the end of the notice period and used her emergency fund to pay all the unexpected costs of moving.

Having an emergency fund saved meant that Shayna was able to avoid getting into more debt: she didn't have to use her credit card, and she dealt with the emergency without stressing about the costs. She is now working on topping her emergency fund back up.

9

INVESTING

When you think about investments, you might think about stocks and shares and men in suits. The last bit is total nonsense: investing your money is a central part of your money management toolkit, and it's something you can start to do right now. It's especially important for Black women to invest, to start addressing the very real issue of the racial wealth gap within the UK. Women of colour are heavily impacted by the intersection of the gender pay gap and the ethnicity pay gap, and investing gives us the opportunity to make our money work for us. Don't wait for the powers that be to close the gap. We need to start investing right now.

If the idea of investing money is new to you, it simply means allocating your money to a particular place in the hope of receiving a profitable return after a period of time.

Profit can come in the form of interest gained or an increase in the value of your investment – or both. A helpful way of thinking about investing is to consider the investments you make in other things, such as your relationship, education or fitness. You put time and energy into these aspects of your life, with the intention of getting a positive return. The same applies to any money you invest. But – just like how no matter how much you invest in a relationship, the other person may never return your feelings – returns on investments are never guaranteed. Sometimes you get back less than you put in, and sometimes you come out on top. Investing is an inherently risky aspect of money management, and all investment products carry a clear warning of this. As an investor, you need to understand that some risk is always involved, but the good news is that you can find out what level you feel comfortable with and only invest in funds that are suitable for your attitude to risk. In other words, you can take steps to mitigate the risk.

The element of risk is one of the factors that differentiates investing from savings. If you put money into a savings account with a 0.2% interest rate, you are guaranteed to receive that interest rate each year, whereas you can't reliably predict the profit you'll make on an investment. This might make you think that you may as well stick to savings accounts, but I urge you to seriously consider otherwise.

While it's great to receive interest on your savings and it's important to save money, the reality is the current interest rates are unlikely to beat the rate of inflation – which is 0.2% at the time of writing.

Inflation means the general increase in prices and fall in the purchasing value of money. When inflation is high, everyday goods become more expensive and the value of your currency is slowly eroded, so if your savings interest rate does not increase in line with inflation, your spending power on the same goods and services will decrease. For example, a year ago I was able to purchase three plantains from the market for £1, but now those same three plantains cost £1.50. This is just a small example of inflation (which in this case is an extortionate 50%). In real life, the rate of inflation can skyrocket. Think about house prices in the UK: in 1950, the average house cost £2,000. Today the average UK house price is £232,749.* Inflation has a very real impact on buying power. It means that if your salary isn't increasing at the same rate as inflation, you're going to be in trouble – fast.

Which brings us back to investing. Unlike saving, investing allows us to beat the rate of inflation due to the

---

* https://www.ons.gov.uk/economy/inflationandpriceindices/ bulletins/housepriceindex/july2020

higher returns involved. According to data collected by Goldman Sachs, the average return on investing money in the US stock market for ten years has been 9.2%* – so, while investing is certainly riskier than saving and requires you to tie up your money for a while, it's a vital way to increase your personal wealth. When you do start investing, it is important to note that you will have to pay either monthly fees or a fee per transaction. Any website or app you use for investing will show the fees, and will log what you are investing and how much you're paying. Another great resource that has an investment fee calculator is the Boring Money website, which I've included a link to in the 'Helpful websites' section at the back.

Don't be put off by the terms 'stock market' or 'stock exchange'. The stock market is where people can buy and sell shares in companies. Stock exchanges used to just be physical places – think of Wall Street or London Stock Exchange – but now they're also online so anyone can buy shares through them. Not all companies are listed on the stock exchange; in order to be listed, a company must go public (which means that people can buy shares in that company).

---

* https://www.businessinsider.com/personal-finance/average-stock-market-return

A share is one of the equal parts into which a company's capital is divided. When you buy a share, you have a stake in that company's success – or failure. You buy shares in the hope that the share price will increase (due to the company performing well). If you buy shares at a lower price than the price you sell them for, you've made a profit. If the company is doing well and they pay shareholders a dividend, you have made another profit from your shares.

Some people like to try to predict which companies are on the up, so they can buy shares more cheaply and sell them on after making a profit. If you invest all your money in one company and the business performs badly, your share price will drop significantly and you will lose money (don't put all your eggs in one basket!). Instead, it's wise to buy shares in multiple companies. One way to mitigate risk is to build a diversified portfolio containing a number of different shares from a range of sectors, such as utilities, technology, telecommunications, finance and healthcare.

Another way to mitigate risk is to hold on to your shares for a long time – at the minimum, for five years or longer. This is because share prices go up and down every day, so holding shares for the long term will allow time for the highs to even out the lows. Also, the longer you keep your shares, the more you will benefit from the power of compound interest.

Compounding is a beautiful thing: it essentially means that your money is working for you, as you're earning interest on top of interest. For example, if you have invested £100 in shares that pay 10% interest per annum, at the end of Year 1 you will have £110. The following year, you will gain another 10% of interest on the £110 you now have, so at the end of Year 2 you will have £121; at the end of Year 3, you'll have £133.10; at the end of Year 4 you'll have £146.41. In just four years, you will have made a profit of almost 50% on your original investment. If you reinvest any dividend payments you earn on shares and buy more shares, and the share price increases over time, this has a similar compounding effect on your investment over the long term.

So, how do you start investing? The good news is, it's never been easier. Previously, investing had to be done over the phone or in a broker's office, but today that formality has gone out of the window and all barriers to entry have been removed. Before you get started, make sure you do a financial health check. Do you have any high-interest debts? If so, you should think about clearing them before jumping into investing, because the cost of the debt could be more than the return you make. Have you got an emergency fund? Remember, it's super important to have a buffer so if anything happens, your financial plan is not thrown into chaos. Are you in a position to tie up some money for at least five years? If you think you will need money in the shorter term, a cash ISA may be a better option, as it will allow you to access your money if needed. Investing is for everyone, but only at the right time. It all depends on your individual circumstances.

If you're good to go, then there are several ways to start investing. You can invest as little as £1 using apps such as Trading 212 or Freetrade. When I started, I invested £50 per month in mutual funds/index funds through Hargreaves Lansdown. Here are some of the many apps and websites you could check out:

Moneybox
Nutmeg
Wealthify
Plum
Wealthsimple
Moneyfarm
Acorns
E*trade
interactive investor/Share.com (they have joined forces)
Vanguard

This is not a complete list and there are always new apps entering the market, but these are a great way to get started. Do your research: you could start with an app that provides a level of free investing, i.e. zero fees to begin with, or one that provides a dummy trial environment. Start small then increase the amount you invest. As you start to pay off your debt, perfect your side hustle, earn more income from work or a second job or receive bonuses, you could invest this money. Remember, you're on a mission to grow your investments and upgrade your financial lifestyle.

If you want to start investing larger sums of money, I recommend you consult an independent financial adviser. They will look at all your financial circumstances and help you to establish the level of risk you're comfortable with when it comes to investing. Alternatively, you can access a robo-adviser online, which will ask you questions about your risk tolerance and investment timeline and suggest options for you based on your answers. Robo-advisers use algorithms to decide what you should invest in, based on the answers you give. Because you're not using a human to actively pick funds for you, the costs are lower. You simply add money to your account regularly and the robo-adviser will automatically allocate your money to the chosen fund.

Please note: robo-advisers are sometimes criticised because they do not offer a personalised service, like one you would receive from a financial adviser. If your requirements become more complex or the sum of money you want to invest increases, this may not be the best option for you.

CASE STUDY: INVESTING

Client: Morgan

Morgan called me because she was interested in learning more about investing. She had saved into a cash ISA for a long time so had savings. She had a pension and no debt, and had actually already bought shares in a business a number of years ago, based on a recommendation from a friend. Unfortunately, the value of her shares had plunged.

While I did not give Morgan advice about specific businesses or index funds to invest in, I pointed her towards useful resources so she could carry out her own research and decide what she wanted to invest in. I also spoke to her about my own experience of investing, and gave her details of various platforms available to invest through, the importance of thinking about investing as a long-term commitment and the benefits of having a diversified portfolio.

During our catch-up call a month later, Morgan told me she

had started investing £100 per month into an index fund that tracked the S&P 500. She also had plans to invest in other index funds and asset classes, once she had done more research.

(Please do your own research or speak to an independent financial adviser to decide what investment strategy is best for you.)

Some people feel knowledgeable enough to make their own investment decisions. They choose their own shares to invest in, based on their own analysis of, and research into, the stock market. You might want to do some research into companies you know about, to find out where they sit in the market. Maybe there are industries that you understand and know well? If so, carry out research to see who the solid companies are in that sector. I spent several years working in software, SaaS (software as a service) companies in particular, so I have an interest in the technology sector. Apple, Amazon, Microsoft, Tesla, Zoom, Netflix and Alphabet (Google's parent company) were some of the first shares I looked into, but because they're the behemoths of the tech space they are super expensive (at the time of writing, Amazon's share price is $3,199.20). Luckily, there are several ways to invest without having to have thousands of pounds in the bank.

Fractional shares

Fractional shares enable you to buy a fraction of a share. Through apps such as Freetrade and Trading 212, it's possible to invest in Amazon shares with just £10, which means you own 0.0031257 of an Amazon share. As discussed previously, it's good to diversify your portfolio, so you might spend £100 and choose ten different shares to invest in at £10 each per month. There's nothing stopping you from doing this today.

Index funds

To explain what an index fund is, you first need to understand what a stock market index is. You've probably heard of a few examples of stock market indices (simply the plural of index), such as the FTSE 100, the S&P 500 or the Nasdaq 100. Within each stock market index sits a collection of companies, so it's like having a shopping basket full of shares, and they're usually grouped together based on the following:

Size:	Small, medium or large
Location:	UK, US or emerging markets
Sector:	Business or industry, tech, finance, etc.
Currencies:	Foreign currencies, bonds, stocks

The companies that make up the FTSE 100 index are the 100 largest companies in the UK. Stock market indices are a good way for investors to benchmark the performance of their investment portfolios: if the S&P 500 index goes up by 5% over a year but your portfolio goes down by 3%, it may be time to look at the shares that make up your portfolio to see which shares are causing the downward trend.

Index funds are low-cost, ready-made portfolios of companies that mirror some or all of the companies within a stock market index. Their aim is to match the performance of the index as closely as possible – talk about ready-made diversification! If you invest in an index fund, you could be investing in up to 3,000 companies (some index funds cover worldwide companies). Whichever fund you choose, you own a small portion of each company.

Index funds have several benefits, such as a low barrier to entry (some funds have no minimum investment requirements). Some also have no fees, although the majority will, so be aware of this. Analysing the value of individual companies takes a lot of time, and investing in index funds saves you from having to do this.

All good? Right, now it's time to get started. First, decide how you want to invest. Do you want to choose the shares yourself? Do you want a ready-made portfolio? Do you want to speak to an adviser and get their recommendations? If you decide to go down the DIY route, it's important to do your research before you choose which platform, app or website to use. If you opt to speak to a financial adviser, you might use websites such as Unbiased or the Chartered Institute for Securities & Investment's wayfinder tool to find one (see the 'Helpful websites' section at the back of the book).

If these more traditional types of investing don't appeal, or if you want to diversify your investment portfolio even more, then there are other asset classes you can invest in as well. Chapter 10 focuses on alternative asset classes but, for now, I hope I've convinced you that investing isn't just for suit-wearing City types. It's for you – and you can get started any time!

One of the best things about investing regularly is knowing not just that I'm saving, but also that I'm making my money work for me. For years I had wanted to invest but, since I never had any spare money, this wasn't possible. Once my finances were in order and I could afford it, the first thing I did was invest. This was the fulfilment of a long-held goal, and it felt so good to finally achieve it. It has created a snowball effect: each year, I have invested more and more – and I can see the results. I can see how well my investments are performing – or not (like I said, there's always a risk involved), and it has been fulfilling teaching myself how to invest.

Will I ever stop investing? No way.

10

ASSETS

You already know what assets are, as you listed your personal assets in Chapter 3, but in case you need a quick refresher, assets are resources that have an economic value (i.e. things you own and could sell). Assets are super important: if you want to grow your finances, you need to create more assets.

Shares are a type of asset, as we buy them in the hope that they will go up in value, and then we will sell them to make a profit. One good way of diversifying your portfolio is to invest in alternative asset classes. When we talk about asset classes, we're simply differentiating between different types of assets. Other asset classes include property, bonds, commodities such as gold, wheat or oil, and businesses. Each asset class has a level of risk, so it's important to

137

consider your risk appetite when you're thinking about other assets to invest in. I'll go through each of these asset classes in this chapter, so you can understand what they're all about.

Bonds

Let's look at the least risky asset class to begin with: bonds. Investing in NS&I Premium Bonds – which are backed by HM Treasury and are 100% secure – effectively involves you lending money to the government and getting an IOU. Each month all Premium Bonds are entered in a prize draw, and if your bonds are picked out, you will win money, from £25 up to £1,000,000. You can encash your bonds at any time.

Large businesses like Microsoft and Tesco also issue bonds. If you buy bonds in these companies, you are lending them money to carry out their projects. Bonds are often referred to as fixed income investments because, when you buy a government or corporate bond, you lend an agreed amount of money for a certain period of time. Once the bond expires (at its maturity date), you will get back your original investment. An investor also benefits from regular payments known as coupons (similar to interest payments), which are usually paid twice per year and are fixed at a percentage of the final maturity payment. For example, an investor could buy a bond for £600 with a maturity date in five years' time. Over those five years they will receive coupon payments of 5% of the value of their investment per annum. At the point of maturity, they also get £1,000 back (this increase in value is your reward for lending the money). That's why bonds are generally regarded as solid investments, because you're guaranteed to receive the lump sum *and* regular payments each year until the bond matures.

Bonds are considered to be a more stable investment than stocks and shares, because governments and large businesses don't tend to default or struggle to pay back loans and coupons. That said, like any investment, bonds are not totally risk-free. Bond prices are impacted by fluctuations in interest rates: as the interest rate increases, bond prices decrease – and vice versa. Let's use the example above. Imagine that, after having the bond for four out of the five years, you wish to sell it on because your financial situation has changed. But, since you purchased the bond four years ago, interest rates have increased, which means that the interest rate paid on newer bonds is higher. Newer bonds, and their higher interest rates, are more attractive to bond buyers, so for your bond to compete and be more attractive, you will need to discount the price of your bond. That means that, rather than selling it for the £600 you paid for it, you may need to sell it for £520 (there are online bond calculators you can use to work out how bond prices are affected by interest rate changes). So, even though investing in bonds is a pretty safe option, it's worth being aware of the potential risks, so you aren't caught out.

One way to mitigate the risk of being impacted by interest rate changes is to diversify your portfolio with a mixture of asset classes. This brings me on to the next one, which is my favourite: property. There are several ways to invest in property – you can buy to let, flip a property or invest in a real estate investment trust (REIT). Here, I'll walk you through the various options.

Property

By-to-let

Buy-to-let property investing is a great opportunity to earn extra income in two ways (if all goes well): (1) from monthly rental income and (2) from an increase in the value of the property over time. This is why it's a great example of an alternative asset class: it creates income right now and in the future. The popularity of Airbnb and staycationing means that lots of people are looking for short-term holiday lets in the UK, so you may have a bigger market than in the past. Quite a few property investors I know started by renting out a room to cover the cost of their mortgage. Why not be creative and think about your options? (Note: over the past three years the UK government has reduced the tax relief available on buy-to-let properties for private landlords, making this a less attractive option. Also, if you make a profit when you sell your buy-to-let property, you'll be liable to pay capital gains tax.*)

---

* A useful link on property investing and the costs involved is: https://www.google.co.uk/amp/s/www.moneyadviceservice.org.uk/ en/articles/buy-to-let-property-investments/amp

Of course, property prices can drop, and there may be times when you have no tenants. At these times, you will need to ensure you can cover all your costs, such as the mortgage, utility bills and council tax. It is important to plan for such eventualities, so consider taking out insurance that covers void periods, and think about whether you can afford to cover the cost of your home and your rental property (depending on how many properties you invest in) if something does go wrong.*

At a recent course I attended, run by the PropElle network, one panellist described how she used an inheritance of £30,000 to grow her property portfolio into hundreds of houses. One of the tips she shared, which will help you cover yourself during bumpy times, was: always try to overpay (even by just £20 or £30 per month) wherever possible on each mortgage. She says doing this helped her to get through periods of recession and tough times in the housing market.

I love discussions like these, because getting into property investing has always been a goal of mine. After I moved in with my partner, I got my old home ready

---

* For more on becoming a landlord, see https://www.which.co.uk/money/mortgages-and-property/buy-to-let/becoming-a-landlord-ak37s4b81j0b

to be let. I won't lie: the process involved some really unexpected (yet essential) steps, such as making sure I had gas and electrical safety certificates and installing the legally required number of smoke alarms, but I threw myself into it and learned a lot along the way. I used a property management company to find tenants – such companies also carry out financial background checks on tenants and manage properties, for a fee. They let me know if the property needs any repairs, and they can provide access to tradespeople if required. This works for me because, while I can tidy, paint and put together flat-pack furniture, I don't live close by and wouldn't be on hand if there was a problem. So, before you invest in a buy-to-let property, consider whether you want to deal directly with your tenants or go through a property management company. If you decide to deal with your tenants directly, be honest with yourself: do you have the time and money available to fix any issues that arise? We've all had bad landlords – don't be one of them.

Flipping houses

Another way to invest in property is to start flipping houses (doesn't it sound ridiculous?). House flipping means buying a house, increasing its value (usually by refurbishing it, making repairs, upgrading the décor and furnishings), then selling it, making a profit. House flipping is usually the quickest way to make a profit on property, because you do the work to improve the property as quickly as possible after buying it, rather than waiting for the value of the property to increase over time. The secret is to do your research. Look at house prices in your local area so you can see if a house is for sale at a bargain price. Check whether any developments are planned that will increase the house price quickly – perhaps a new train station is being built that will make the area super accessible for businesses and families.

Property flippers are typically not in it for the rental income but for the capital gains they can make – and flipping makes for great TV (*Homes Under the Hammer* and *Selling Sunset*, anyone?). After watching a particularly thrilling episode of *Homes Under the Hammer*, I was inspired to attend an open viewing for an auction property not far from where I lived. It was an eye-opening experience. As I walked up the garden (more like overgrown jungle) path to the front door, which had previously been boarded up with metal boards to stop people from gaining access, I realised this wasn't a project for the faint-hearted. I held my breath when I entered, which is just as well, since I'd never seen dirt or dust like it before . . . or since. There was a hole in the upstairs bedroom ceiling and the paintwork was seriously chipped. It was clear that the property had been unloved and unlooked after for some time. However, when I forced myself to use my imagination and see beyond the decrepit state of the property, I could see it had a lot going for it: located in an up-and-coming area with good transport links, schools and thriving businesses, it had the potential to be a lovely family home. I was excited by the prospect, but I knew I wasn't the right investor for the project at the time. It would require a *lot* of work to get it to a habitable standard, and I had neither the experience nor the time to take it on. It was not for me – but I could see the potential.

When it comes to auction properties, it's important to note how different the buying process is from buying through an estate agent. Once the hammer falls at an auction, the contract is binding. You cannot change your mind; you must move forward with the purchase, so you have to be absolutely sure about it. The discounted prices of properties at auction can be really tempting, but you can also source discounted properties through an estate agency. If you have a good relationship with an agent, you could ask them to tell you about new properties before they're marketed online. You can also look out for repossessed properties. I know someone who bought a repossessed property from an estate agent at a discounted price – my mother. The property didn't require much work at all, just some deep cleaning and cosmetic updates.

Flipping properties is a great investment strategy to consider, but you must be mindful of the downsides. Property renovations can take longer than anticipated if you don't know what you're doing or if something unexpected (and expensive) needs to be done out of the blue. Make sure you factor in the cost of all work required as accurately as possible; you don't want to pay more than you will get back in profit when you sell the property. That said, while no investments are without risk, property is a fairly stable place to put your money, as it tends to be unaffected by swings in the stock market and it's always in demand. Just do your research first.

Commercial property and REITs

Another option is investing in commercial property. Real estate investment trusts (REITs) are companies that buy income-producing property, such as hotels, warehouses, self-storage facilities, office buildings, retail centres, serviced apartments and affordable housing. A REIT invests in properties in a similar way that an index fund invests in a selection of stocks and shares. REITs were introduced as a financial product in the UK in 2007 and are extremely popular, because they give investors who may not have the opportunity to purchase a property outright the chance to invest in the property market, and investors can profit from price movements.

You can invest in REITs by buying shares directly in the company itself, in which case you become a shareholder and can receive dividends. Legally REITs are required to pay out at least 90% of their rental income to shareholders. Alternatively, you can buy the shares of multiple REIT companies through a REIT exchange-traded fund, which is essentially a way to track a basket of REIT companies. Investing in REITs is typically part of a long-term investment strategy, due to the yearly dividend payments, so they are often favoured by investors setting up retirement portfolios. It's also much easier than the other two property investment strategies, as it doesn't require you to view or renovate any properties, and you don't have to talk to conveyancing solicitors or deal with mortgage advisers or brokers. You can go online and start investing today through investment brokerage websites and apps mentioned in Chapter 9, such as Hargreaves Lansdown, Freetrade, Wealthify and Wealthsimple. As with any financial product available for investment, you do need to research the performance and financial status of the REIT. There is always a risk that share prices can go down as well as up.

I hope this has given you a quick run-through of the different ways you can invest in property. If none of these property investments suit you or your circumstances, you could consider investing in commodities. This is the catch-all term for the raw materials that are either consumed or used to build other products, such as metals, agricultural products like wheat and soybeans, and energy, such as gas and oil. These commodities are the basic building blocks of the global economy and are traded on exchanges around the world.

Commodities

Investing in commodities is the riskiest option of all because prices fluctuate significantly based on many factors, including supply and demand, economic and political events, and the weather. Gold is often regarded as a 'safe' investment, whereas oil has recently proven more risky. The oil price had crashed before Covid-19 due to falling demand; then during lockdown in spring 2020, the number of cars on the roads dropped dramatically, so there was even less demand for petrol, and the value of crude oil plummeted further.

The cost of buying some physical commodities is very high. To buy a barrel of crude oil or natural gas, consider all the variables required – transportation costs, storage costs, insurance costs, the legal requirements. This makes it prohibitive for the average investor.* However, if you're interested, you can invest directly in commodities through an online brokerage account or you can invest in exchange-traded funds (ETFs). These are like index funds, in that you can invest in an array of companies and commodities, but they can be traded on the stock market. You can buy and sell ETFs like shares on the stock exchanges and you can buy ETFs that focus on various sectors, such as telecoms ETFs, gold ETFs and natural gas ETFs.†

---

* A funny article on the subject: https://www.bloomberg.com/news/articles/2015-11-03/that-time-i-tried-to-buy-some-crude-oil
† A useful website if you want to find out more is https://www.boringmoney.co.uk/learn/articles/what-is-an-etf-and-how-should-i-use-one

The volatility of the stock market means that investing in commodities is risky. Investing through an ETF still comes with a risk, however, it allows you to diversify and exposes you to commodities not previously available at a much lower cost than buying them directly. I suggest you do your research into commodities and ETFs. Think about your risk appetite. An ETF may make up part of a diversified portfolio of investments.

Angel investing

Another asset class I want to tell you about is angel investing. This means investing in a start-up company. You don't necessarily need a lot of money to do this; you can start with just £5,000.* Some businesses that have raised funds recently via a combination of venture capitalists and angel investors are BYP Network, Afrocenchix, Jamii and Black Ballad.

Angel investing is a very risky form of investing. Unlike established businesses, you can't analyse start-ups

---

* See https://www.angelinvestingschool.com/can-i-start-angel-investing-with-just-5k

to assess whether the business is going to be worth your investment. While we all hope to invest in the next Netflix or Tesla, it's worth remembering that 20% of businesses fail in their first year.* However, if you do support a business in its early days and it later floats on the stock market, you're likely to make a pretty good profit.

Bearing in mind the risks, angel investing can be a worthwhile way to put your money to use. You could invest in start-ups owned by Black women, for example. It's very easy to make these investments using apps like Crowdcube and Seedrs, and you can also join networks where angel investors pool their money, discuss investment opportunities and set up meetings with founders of start-ups. This kind of collaboration isn't something you can get from an app; you can't beat talking to someone face to face to decide whether you think the company's founder can move the business forward.

---

* https://www.forbes.com/sites/briannawiest/2020/01/24/small-businesses-that-fail-in-the-first-year-always-have-these-3-things-in-common/#2a79fac326c7

Starting your own business

Setting up a business is not easy, and may not suit everyone, but if you enjoy working independently, are self-motivated, and have a really good idea for a new business, then it may work for you. Here are some websites you may find useful:

- https://www.bl.uk/business-and-ip-centre
- https://www.princes-trust.org.uk//help-for-young-people/support-starting-business
- https://entrepreneurhandbook.co.uk/starting-a-business
- https://www.moneyadviceservice.org.uk/en/articles/thinking-of-starting-up-in-business
- https://minutehack.com/guides/how-do-you-know-youre-the-right-type-of-person-to-start-a-business

There are plenty of books available that tell you how to start your own business, so I won't go into more detail here.

The risks and benefits of investing

Before investing in any asset classes, it is important to think about the risks and benefits, so you can make smart investment decisions based on your own circumstances. Someone who is very risk-averse may decide to steer clear of a portfolio full of risky asset classes, for example. Also, if you're nearing retirement, now is probably not the time to choose higher-risk investment opportunities. A balanced approach that takes into consideration your risk appetite, your age (because longevity tends to even out any potential for volatility) and personal circumstances is best.

CONCLUSION

Although this is primarily a book about money, starting to think about looking after your finances and creating a money management plan for yourself is a tough exercise in self-exploration and personal growth. Looking at your internal money mindset isn't easy, and it can be difficult to examine the influence of the people who raised you, own your personal blind spots and admit to struggling financially. But whatever has happened in the past, you can change the way you handle money. I'm proof of this. I didn't save a penny for ten years or have a clue about investing, and now I save and invest every month. So, whether you're currently where you want to be with money, or you believe there's room for improvement, please feel encouraged, because I have been privileged to see – and help – hundreds of women turn their finances around.

We know that Black women face a double whammy when it comes to the gender and ethnicity pay gaps. There is a lot of work to be done to combat wider inequalities, not just in the UK but globally, and we're unlikely to see a great levelling-up in our lifetime – and maybe not even in our children's lifetime. This pains me, but I'm comforted by the unapologetic, ambitious and money-minded women I have the good fortune to meet daily. We are a force to be reckoned with, and the sooner we realise and appreciate our own worth, the more likely we are to start seeing changes.

Numerous organisations have also inspired me, by not only highlighting structural inequalities but also providing suggestions for how these can be eradicated. I appreciate everything the Runnymede Trust, the World Economic Forum, the United Nations Entity for Gender Equality and the Empowerment of Women (also known as UN Women) and the Fawcett Society have done to shake things up. Be reassured that these organisations are out there championing us – but also remember that *you* can be the change-maker for yourself and your circle. Change can start here, with you.

In spite of the challenges you face, I hope that you finish this book with a better, more positive money mindset and can use your new knowledge to move forward on your financial journey. This book is not about getting rich quick; it's about giving you financial peace of mind and improving your money management skills. You can apply this toolkit of strategies and methods to your finances so you can correct any money mistakes you've made and improve your financial future.

As I said at the beginning, it's high time we all started making our hard-earned money work even harder for us.

RECOMMENDED READING

Books

Clever Girl Finance by Bola Sokunbi (Wiley, 2019)

How to Save It by Bola Sol (Merky Books, 2021)

Money: A User's Guide by Laura Whateley (Fourth Estate, 2018)

Real Money Answers for Every Woman by Patrice C. Washington (HarperCollins, 2016)

Rich Dad Poor Dad by Robert T. Kiyosaki (Plata Publishing, 2017)

Sheconomics by Karen J. Pine and Simonne Gnessen (Headline, 2009)

Smart Women Finish Rich by David Bach (Pisces Books, 2018)

The Intelligent Investor by Benjamin Graham (Harper Business, 2003)

The Richest Man in Babylon by George S. Clason (Berkley, 2008)

Think and Grow Rich by Napoleon Hill (Tarcherperigee, 2016)

You are a Badass at Making Money by Jen Sincero (John Murray Learning, 2018)

You're Not Broke You're Pre-Rich by Emilie Bellet (Cassell, 2019)

Helpful websites

www.pension-tracing-service-uk.co.uk – a website that helps you trace lost pensions.

www.pensionbee.com/pension-calculator – if you're unsure how much you should be saving for retirement, use this pension calculator to find out.

www.moneyadviceservice.org.uk/en/tools/pension-calculator – if you're unsure how much you should be saving for retirement, use this pension calculator to find out.

www.gov.uk/plan-for-retirement – a government site where you can check what pensions and financial support you're eligible for.

www.gov.uk/check-state-pension – find out how much

state pension you could get, when you can get it, and how to increase it, if you can.

www.boringmoney.co.uk/calculator – find out how much you will pay in fees in various types of investment.

www.unbiased.co.uk – find qualified financial advisers, mortgage brokers and accountants here.

www.financialplanning.org.uk/wayfinder/tips-tools – a free series of money guides, and a resource for finding financial advisers.

www.blackgirlfinance.co.uk – the financial coaching company for Black women in the UK.

www.moneyadviceservice.org.uk/en/tools/debt-advice locator – get free debt advice here.

www.citizensadvice.org.uk/debt-and-money – Citizens Advice is a network of independent charities that offer confidential, impartial advice online, over the phone and in person, for free.

www.gov.uk/find-coronavirus-support – if you've been affected by Covid-19, find out here what support available to you.

www.blackpropertynetwork.com – Black Property network's aim is to help people in the Black community to take charge of their financial situation and in UK property.

www.brickzwithtipz.co.uk – contains a wealth of advice on how to invest in property.

www.propellenetwork.com – the PropElle network is a community investment network for women.

Remarkable women in finance

Bola Sol, the founder of Rich Girl Chronicles, creator of the platform Refined Currency, author of *How to Save It* and host of the Bola Sol Show, is an inspiring entrepreneur. She is a personal wellness coach, and creates great conversations around women and money. https://www. instagram.com/bola_sol

Tonya Rapley is a millennial money expert, always on Instagram with inspirational money content. Check out her website for posts and podcasts about money management. https://myfabfinance.com

Bola Sokunbi is the creator of the Clever Girl Finance platform, the book of the same name and the recently released book, *Clever Girl Finance: Learn how investing works, Grow your money.* Her personal finance journey is inspiring. https://www.clevergirlfinance.com

Emilie Bellet is the creator of the Vestpod platform. Emilie is always shining a light on financial inequality and her workshops, which cover various topics, such as investing and women in the workplace, are highly recommended. https://www.vestpod.com

Jen Sincero's book, *You are a Badass at Making Money*, is highly recommended. It's a fantastic book about money and mindset. https://www.jensincero.com

Davinia Tomlinson, the founder of Rainchq, is on a mission to promote greater financial inclusion for women by closing the gender investing gap. Her platform encourages investing and well-being – I'm a big fan. https://www.rainchq.com

Patrice Washington has been on an amazing financial journey. After losing everything in the financial crash of 2008, she has picked her finances back up – and she now helps other women to do the same. She is all about creating wealth in a holistic sense, not just financially. https://www.patricewashington.com

Tiffany Aliche, founder of the Budgetnista and the Live Richer Academy, is dedicated to making life-changing financial education accessible to women globally. She is known as America's favourite financial educator. https://www.instagram.com/thebudgetnista

Jennifer Kempson, YouTuber, blogger, author, mentor and coach, is a powerhouse at helping others thrive with their money. https://www.mamafurfur.com

Francesca Henry founded the Money Fox platform. Her candour and honesty when talking about her financial journey are super refreshing. She also provides great resources about earning extra money and paying down debt. https://www.themoneyfox.com

ACKNOWLEDGEMENTS

Writing this book has been a journey – like raising a child, it really does take a village to write a book!

To my family and friends, who were so understanding when I had the idea for Black Girl Finance and gave me the time and space to write – thank you for always being supportive.

To my editor Alison MacDonald and the Quercus team: when I received your email, I was equally terrified and excited, but I am so grateful that you have been able to share my vision and work with me to bring it to life. Thank you.

And lastly, to the Black Girl Finance community. Your enthusiasm when I announced my book was out of this world. You were – and continue to be – my inspiration, so thank you. Keep being the unapologetic, ambitious, money-minded women you are.